Johann Wolfgang von Goethe, John Stuart Blackie

The WISDOM of GOETHE

Johann Wolfgang von Goethe, John Stuart Blackie

The WISDOM of GOETHE

ISBN/EAN: 9783741122835

Manufactured in Europe, USA, Canada, Australia, Japa

Cover: Foto ©Andreas Hilbeck / pixelio.de

Manufactured and distributed by brebook publishing software (www.brebook.com)

Johann Wolfgang von Goethe, John Stuart Blackie

The WISDOM of GOETHE

THE
WISDOM OF GOETHE

BY

JOHN STUART BLACKIE

EMERITUS PROFESSOR OF GREEK IN THE
UNIVERSITY OF EDINBURGH

WILLIAM BLACKWOOD AND SONS
EDINBURGH AND LONDON
MDCCCLXXXIII

TO THE

REV. WALTER CHALMERS SMITH, D.D.

A LARGE-HEARTED PREACHER,

A GENEROUS THEOLOGIAN,

AND A HEALTHY-MINDED POET,

THIS MANUAL OF WISE WORDS,

FOR GUIDANCE IN FRUITFUL ACTION

AND SOUND THINKING,

Is Dedicated

BY HIS OLD FRIEND

THE EDITOR.

CONTENTS.

	PAGE
PREFACE,	ix
CHRONOLOGICAL SUMMARY OF GOETHE'S LIFE,	xvii
ESTIMATE OF THE CHARACTER OF GOETHE,	xxi
LIFE, CHARACTER, AND MORALS,	1
RELIGION,	55
POLITICS,	93
LITERATURE—POETRY,	107
PHILOSOPHY, METAPHYSICS, LOGIC, TRUTH, AND SCIENCE,	149
NATURE—NATURAL HISTORY,	179
ART,	199
WOMEN,	223
EDUCATION AND CULTURE,	233

PREFACE.

THERE is nothing fills me with more sorrow occasionally than to see how foolishly some people throw away their lives. It is a noble thing to live; at least a splendid chance of playing a significant game — a game which we may never have the chance to play again, and which it is surely worth the while to try to play skilfully; to bestow at least as much pains upon as many a one does on billiards or lawn-tennis. But these pains are certainly not always given; and so the game of life is lost, and the grand chance of forming a manly character is gone; for no man can play a game well who leaves his moves to chance; and so, instead of fruitful victories, brilliant blunders are all the upshot of what many a record of distinguished lives has to present. The only remedy for this evil that I know is to impress on young men with all seriousness that life, though a pleasant thing, is no joke; and that, if they will go to sea without chart, compass, or pilot, they have a fair chance to be wrecked. But who is to impress such a lesson? Some name with authority, of course; for the individual, like the great world, is governed, as Goethe well says, by wisdom, by authority, and by show; and, though wisdom is wisely put first in this triad of directing powers, it is on authority that the great masses of men have to rely, when they look out, as they must do, in nine cases out of ten, for a guidance outside of their own experience; for authority is the form that wisdom must always take, before it can be generally recognised and become permanently influential. Now every age has its own authority, as in other regions, so specially in the domain of the conduct of life; and in the present age I have found no name whose utterances have a better chance to be generally accepted than the great German poet-thinker, Johann Wolfgang von Goethe. His wisdom is generally acknowledged, even by those who entertain the most unfavourable views of his character: and having, in my own personal experience, had reason to thank God that at an early period of my life I became acquainted with the writings of this great man, it occurred to me that I could do no better service to the intelligent youth of this generation, for whose benefit it has been my duty and my pleasure to work through a long life, than to lay before them in a systematic form his most significant dicta on the important problems of sound thinking and noble living. In doing this I had as my starting-point that admirable book, Eckermann's Conversations with Goethe; which I believe I was the first to introduce to the British public, some forty or fifty years ago, in the pages of the 'Foreign Quarterly Review,' and which has since found its way extensively into English hands, through the translation of Mr Oxenford. Next to that, invaluable stores were found in the 'Reflexionen und Maximen,' in the papers entitled 'Gott, Gemüth, und Welt,' the 'Venetian Epigrams,' the 'Weissagungen des Bakis,' and 'The Four Seasons.' Among the larger works, my principal extracts were made from 'Wilhelm Meister's Lehrjahre and Wanderjahre,' from the 'Wahlverwandtschaften,' from 'Faust,' 'Tasso,' 'Iphigenia,' and the 'Natürliche Tochter,' 'Hermann and Dorothea,' and the 'West-Eastern Divan.'[1] Spe-

[1] From the article in 'Blackwood's Magazine,' December 1882, by J. S. B.

cial aid also I derived from the well-known and valuable collections of Lancizolle,[1] as also from 'Goethe as Naturforscher,' by Meding: Dresden, 1861.

It was my desire in putting this little work before the public to leave the great poet to state his own case, and to make that impression on the unbiassed reader which words of true wisdom flowing into the soul, like healthy breezes into free lungs, naturally make. But I soon became aware that, in the case of Goethe, few unbiassed readers were likely to be found on this side of the Channel; and I could not conceal from myself the fact that the good impression to be made by the wise words of the preacher might be seriously neutralised by the bad impression they entertained of his character. If it has been the good fortune of some great men to have had their virtues brought forward into the foreground, studiously dressed out and magnified, while their vices are cast into the shade and for-

---

[1] (1.) 'Geistesworte aus Goethe's Briefen und Gesprächen:' Berlin, 1853.

(2.) 'Geistesworte aus Goethe's Werken;' second enlarged edition: Berlin, 1860. This is the book with regard to which Bunsen wrote: "Pray read Goethe's 'Geistesworte;' *they are prodigious!*"

(3.) 'Über Goethe's Verhältniss zu Religion und Christenthum:' Berlin, 1855.

gotten or forgiven, no less certainly has the reputation of others suffered from their faults having been prominently flaunted before the public eye, not seldom exaggerated into gross vices, while their no less real virtues were ignored or explained away. This unfortunate fate seems to have followed Goethe, at least under the action of English optics. The judgments which I constantly hear in this country pronounced on the character of this great man always recall to me a story illustrative of a certain style of criticism, which I picked up many years ago from Coleridge's 'Biographia Litteraria.' Two English young gentlemen, fresh from college, and brimful of conceit, as is natural in such creatures, were contemplating Dannecker's well-known sculpture of "Bacchus and Ariadne," one of the principal lions in Frankfurt-on-the-Mayne. Says the one to the other, "What do you think of that, Bill?" to which Bill forthwith, putting his eye-glass to his eye, and thereafter looking up knowingly, replied, "I think it is d—mned like Stilton cheese," pointing, by this remark, to a certain blue streak in the marble which unfortunately had revealed itself, not till the work was too far advanced to allow of a replacement. Besides this easy habit of an assumed superiority, so natural to empty minds, there is in the case of Goethe the unquestioned fact of a great gap between the English and the German mind, which even Englishmen of large culture and high principle find it difficult to overbridge. The Englishman — and I include my brother the Scot here under the general name—is characteristically a man of action, not of contemplation. As such he puts forth his force emphatically in certain definite lines, within which the idea after which he is striving must realise itself: this makes his habit of mind rather constitutional than philosophical, his religion more ecclesiastical than spiritual, his statesmanship guided more by external expediency than by internal principle; and above all things he is a denouncer of sentiment, enthusiasm, and what Napoleon called ideology. The German is the reverse of all this. He is cosmopolitan in his range, contemplative in his habit, and emotional in his temper. The eager struggle of political parties, into which the Englishman puts so much of his moral life, to a thoughtful German makes itself felt as a disturbing force; while the delicate blossoms of the emotional and æsthetical element in our nature, which the Englishman denounces as sentimentality, the German cherishes as a luxury and cultivates as a religion. Two such opposite types of national character, as soon as they come near enough to provoke a mutual estimate, naturally produce a clash: and in this way the English, who in their days of intellectual isolation—days yet fresh in the memory of living men—gloried in simply despising the Germans, now that the current of events has brought with it a general necessity of international recognition, too often make this recognition through a thick atmosphere of misconception and a strong tincture of prejudice. I therefore thought it my duty, in justice both to my author and to my readers, to pave the way for the reception of his sage maxims and wise warnings, by a short estimate of his character as a man and a citizen. This I have done with all patience; and—though I hope in the main with that warm sympathy and kindly appreciation without which all critical estimates are null—at the same time with a determination to blink no ugly questions, and to whitewash no offences which it was impossible to deny.

I intended at one time to have added a short biographical sketch of the poet's life; but considering how well this field has been already worked by Mr Lewes, and in a more portable form by Mr

Hayward,[1] the accomplished translator of 'Faust,' as also in an English translation of Duenzer's life of the poet, at present being issued by Macmillan, I have thought it unnecessary to swell this little volume with any matter of this kind. I have only, therefore, added a short chronological view of the poet's life, divided into its great distinctive periods with a few synchronistic names, which may be useful for many readers, living as they do at the distance of more than a century and a quarter from the date of the poet's birth.

In conclusion, let me return my warm thanks to Messrs Chapman & Hall, Piccadilly, and Messrs George Bell & Sons, York Street, Covent Garden, London, for the handsome manner in which they have allowed me to use Carlyle's translation of 'Wilhelm Meister,' and Oxenford's 'Conversations of Eckermann,' for the purposes of this work. All the other extracts, whether in prose or verse, were translated by myself directly from the German.

EDINBURGH, *March* 1883.

---

[1] Foreign Classics for English Readers: Goethe. By A. Hayward. Edinburgh: Blackwood—1878.

CHRONOLOGICAL SUMMARY

OF

GOETHE'S LIFE.

I.

BIRTH AND BOYHOOD.

Born at Frankfurt-on-the-Mayne,	1749
Seven Years' War—Frederick II.,	1756
Birth of Schiller and Robert Burns,	1759

II.

STUDENTSHIP.

Leipzig University, . . .	1765
Maria Theresa and Joseph II., . .	1765
Strasburg—Cuvier and Wellington born, .	1769
Sesenheim — Frederika — Birth of Wordsworth and Sir W. Scott, .	1770-71

III.
LAW AND LITERATURE.

Wetzlar—Lotte—Coleridge born,	1772
'Götz von Berlichingen,' . .	1773
'Werther'—Robert Southey born,	1774
Lili, . . .	1775

IV.
THE WEIMARIAN APPRENTICESHIP.

Karl August—Frau von Stein, . . .	1775-76
Public business — Court service — Various minor works — Gradual growth of his great classical works, . .	1776-85

V.
ITALY.

'Iphigenia'—'Egmont,'	1787

VI.
MARRIAGE AND DOMESTICATION.

Christiana Vulpius—Byron born, . .	1788
French Revolution — 'Roman Elegies'— 'Tasso,'	1789
Prussian campaign in France—'Optics,'	1792

VII.

SCHILLER AND GOETHE.

Correspondence with Schiller, . . .	1794
'Venetian Epigrams'—'Comparative Anatomy,'	1795
'Hermann and Dorothea,' . . .	1797
'Optics,'	1800
Benvenuto Cellini—'The Natural Daughter,'	1803
Death of Schiller, . . .	1805

VIII.

POLITICAL TROUBLES.

Battle of Jena, . .	1806
'Faust,'	1806
'Elective Affinities'—Tennyson born,	1809
Liberation War, ...	1813
'West-Eastern Divan,' . .	1814-15
Battle of Waterloo, . . .	1815
Natural Science and Morphology, .	1820
'W. Meister's Wanderjahre,' . . .	1821
Various literary, critical, and artistical works,	1822-31
Second Part of 'Faust'—Death of Sir W. Scott,	1831
Death, March 22, ...	1832
Death of Cuvier, ...	1832

ESTIMATE

OF THE

CHARACTER OF GOETHE

—

"*Voilà un homme!*"—Napoleon.

ESTIMATE

OF THE

CHARACTER OF GOETHE.

———•♦•———

I. THE elements and forces that build up a man's genius and form his atmosphere and his environment are of two kinds, internal and external. The internal are what we popularly call his talents and capacities, his intellectual strength, his emotional sensibility, his volitional force, his muscular force, his power of endurance, his self-control, his moral courage, and suchlike; the external factor is composed of the moulding and plastic influences of the family, the Church, the school, the State, the society, the country and climate. The race to which a man belongs, and the nationality out of which he grows, are in some sense part of both factors; for partly, as being bred in the bone and nourished in the blood, they are a constituent element of the individual, helping to make him what he is; partly they may be considered as a sort of atmosphere which he breathes, but which is distinct from the individual self. The internal forces which constitute the individual are of course the strongest and the most emphatically pronounced in those exceptional characters whom history notes as great men; for it is precisely the inherent and original force of their character which makes them great, and places them so far above the masses of the aggregate to which they belong, that they may often not unjustly boast that they have created the circumstances of which they who follow them become the slaves: for always and everywhere the characters of men must be moulded to a great extent by the circumstances, moral and physical, which surround them, against which a certain reactive and plastic force from within will be put forth in direct proportion to the active energy and self-assertive virtue of the individual. Viewed in this aspect we shall find that, while in respect of racial characteristics and national character Goethe was pre-eminently a representative German—as distinctively a German as Voltaire was a Frenchman[1] and So-

[1] To Lewes's remark that Goethe is "more Greek than German," Mr Hutton (Essays, ii. 76) makes the discriminating comment, that "what Lewes had in view was the

crates a Greek—he was at the same time possessed of such singularly original force and rich completeness of character as to have led his people over from a state of feebleness and dependence on foreign influences into a state of firmly rooted native growth, luxuriant blossom, and beneficent fruitage. Of course he was not alone, nor even first in this great work, as the names of Lessing, Klopstock, Wieland, Herder, and others sufficiently show. But he was unquestionably the great master-builder, without whom the edifice of German intellectuality could never have received that homage of general European admiration which has from the commencement of the present century been so willingly or unwillingly conceded.

II. So far as topographical influences could help to make a great German man, Goethe was in the highest degree favoured in having Frankfurt for his birthplace. Politically and historically that city was to Germany what London is to Eng-

heathen element in his character, while his cast of mind is strikingly and distinctively German, far more than Schiller's." This is true; but perhaps Lewes had also in view the form and tone of the 'Iphigenia,' 'Tasso,' and 'Hermann and Dorothea,' which seem to find their prototypes in Sophocles and Homer, rather than in any modern poetical works. It must be borne in mind also that Goethe's character penetrates his works as deeply as his genius commands them.

land, or Edinburgh to Scotland. Time-hallowed memories of famous emperors of European significance, from Charlemagne down to Rudolph of Hapsburg and Maria Theresa, haunted its quaint old streets, and inscribed its gilded rolls; picturesque processions of provosts and pipers, and municipal horsemen in medieval garb, proclaimed the annual gathering of its fair, where the vendors of the most various wares from East and West spread forth the products of their several countries to the public gaze, and fed the imagination of the curious and intelligent youth of the place with the vision of a richly peopled and variously cultured world, outside the narrow bounds of their German home. In respect of society it presented as various and freely pulsing a world as could be found in Germany in that age of political decadence and impending reconstitution; in respect of the beauties of nature and the charms of landscape, if surpassed in sublimity and picturesqueness by some other notable towns of the richly varied Fatherland, it was far removed from the monotonous flatness of Berlin and Munich, and had green wealth enough, either in its immediate vicinity or within easy reach, to satisfy the æsthetical demands of a healthy appetite.

III. In respect of parentage Goethe furnishes a

strong proof of the remark that men of great genius have generally, if not always, been the product of sound and well-conditioned parents. Goethe's father and mother were both in many respects above par; and, like Marcus Antoninus in his diary, he has gratefully recorded the special good gifts and qualities which he received by inheritance from his parents.[1] From his father he received a musculine seriousness of intellect, and a severe love of order in all things; from his mother, qualities even more valuable—a freshness of spirit, a cheerfulness of temper, a capacity of enjoyment, a vivid fancy, a fluent tongue, a firm trust in God, a habitual avoidance of all fret about the past or anxiety about the future, and a courageous grappling with the task of the hour.[2]

IV. In his education he was peculiarly happy,

[1] *Vom Vater hab' ich die Statur,*
Des Lebens ernstes Führen;
Vom Mütterchen die Frohnatur
Und Lust zu fabuliren.

which we may render thus:—

My goodly frame and earnest soul,
I from my sire inherit;
My happy heart and glib discourse,
Was my brave mother's merit.

[2] *Frau Rath:* Briefwechsel von Katharin Elizabeth Goethe. Von Robert *Keil.* Leipzig: 1871.

as his intelligent and well-educated parents took that living interest in it, which, when accompanied with sense and moderation, always makes father and mother the best of schoolmasters. Under their kindly hands, besides the traditional orthodoxy of Latin and Greek, he became early familiar with French and English, and particularly Italian, for which language his father—and the son after him —had a special preference, and which he cultivated not only for its literature, but in connection with the works of ancient and modern art, of which Italy had always been the storehouse and the nursery. It need scarcely be remarked that this early familiarity with ancient and modern languages in the hand of such a highly endowed youth could not fail to be of singular use in widening his range of thought beyond narrow local influences; while it gave him a ready key of entrance into the larger world, where is found the only remedy for those limitations of thought, inadequacies of sentiment, and awkwardnesses of manner, from which home-bred youths are never wholly free.

V. When Goethe, at the age of seventeen, was sent to the University of Leipzig, as a student of law,—a profession which had been chosen for him by his father, rather than dictated by his own genius,—his destiny as a poet, a literary man, a philosopher, a man of science, and an artist—for all this lay in him—became sufficiently manifest. On a temperament keenly alive and delicately sensitive all round to every touch of human sympathy, social attractions and personal charms acted more strongly than academical lectures or critical dissertations; philosophy, general history, natural history, anatomy, art, anything rather than the cold abstractions and bloodless formalisms of law, were tasted and assimilated, as opportunity might offer or appetite invite; but to be laced up in the Spanish boots of any systematic course of prescribed reading, in scholastic fashion, was utterly abhorrent to the large freedom, innate spontaneity, and electric sensibility of the young poet.[1] High original talent, capable of stirring deeply the best

[1] Of course it is obvious that the free range of spontaneous impulse which may be the only sure guidance of a youth of strongly pronounced original genius, might be the ruin of commonplace persons, who demand an external law to complement the deficiencies of their natural character; at the same time, I believe there is no greater error in the training of youth than to proceed on the principle that nothing should be spontaneously evolved, and everything externally imposed on the opening mind. The multiplication of examinations, one of the marked tendencies of the educational features of the age, has a strong tendency to overload the appetite, while it demands only a stimulant, and to cramp the intellect which craves for expansion.

instincts of a poetical nature, is no doubt frequently to be found in the Chairs of the German universities; but at Leipzig, in the days of his undergraduateship, the academical representatives of a flat century had not attained that stature which could have enabled them to exercise any permanent influence on such a lusty young Titan as Wolfgang Goethe—who was accordingly left in a great measure to himself, and that healthy interchange of thought and feeling with well-conditioned young persons of both sexes, which is, after all, the atmosphere most favourable to juvenile development.

VI. The quick and ready sensibility of a nature open at all pores to every human sympathy, which we have just noticed in this young student, was the most potent factor in the formation of his character; a sensibility not only on the emotional side, expanding into loves and friendships of the most rich and varied character, but in its intellectual action also stretching forth feelers of the most many-sided sympathy, appropriation, and assimilation. He was not, like some men of fine genius, a dainty feeder, with a confined range of taste and a broad sweep of aversions: but, as a man with a stout stomach, though he well knew to discriminate good from bad, yet he could enjoy and digest many things; and refused systematically to pamper himself on a few favourite dainties of sentiment, which by repeated action might weaken the digestive faculty it seemed to refine. Hence he could never either think, or feel, or act independently of his environment; and his course of activity, though radically, no doubt, proceeding from what he was, depended in each individual case on where he was. His was a nature to learn from everybody, and to be touched by everything; he had "a grand zest of living";[1] and put forth loving arms in all directions freely, in order to live largely. The present, as he says, had always a most powerful influence upon him: and it were well for all of us if it were more so; for the present moment is all that we can use in the full enjoyment of our vitality; the present opportunity, if not utilised while it lasts, is gone for ever; of the past, memory, with all its magic, can only present us with the dimmest shadows—while he who lives much in the future lives largely in dreams which never can be realised, or in anticipations which may often be disappointed. This broad and many-sided receptiveness of mental constitution brought Goethe at an early period of his career into connection with men of the most various and opposite characters; men very different from himself, but in

[1] Crabb Robinson's Diary, vol. i. chap. xviii.

whom he could always find something to enjoy, and something to learn. Such men were Herder, Jung Stilling, Lavater, Basedow, Jacobi, Merck, and many others. This capacity for friendship, and grateful recognition of everything good and attractive in his fellow-beings, accompanied him through life; and made him, as he advanced in years, the centre to which all the best intellects and the noblest characters in Germany, and not a few beyond the bounds of Fatherland, naturally gravitated. Nor were his sympathies in any case confined to mere human loves and affections. A deep sense of religion, and a profound reverence for hallowed old tradition, were fundamental traits in his character; and, though with no pretensions to orthodoxy, and with more of the artistic Greek than of the Hebrew prophet or the Christian preacher in his temperament, the careful student of his works, not hasty to take offence at isolated passages, will acknowledge in the greatest of German poets the most loving student of the Bible, and the warmest appreciator of the great scope of its teaching. In addition to this he combined a large capacity of vital and social enjoyment with a profound conviction of the seriousness of life, and a sacred regard for the responsibility which the possession of extraordinary talents imposes on those who employ them. Thus richly furnished with all that the largest love and the most loyal reverence can supply to stimulate and to elevate a human soul,[1] he lived and died, not without hard work indeed, and hard struggles, much less untouched by the envy which always waits upon merit, especially in the first steps of its ascent, but in the end emphatically a rich man; rich in friends,[2] rich in love, rich in insight, and rich in good works—the only kind of wealth which a reasonable man should desire to be possessed of in any large quantity.[3]

[1] Crabb Robinson, as above, notes that "in his youth he appears to have had something even of religious enthusiasm," and he would like to know how he lost it. He lost it, as he lost his Wertherian sentimentality, and as all healthy-minded persons lose the high-strained enthusiasms of their youth; but he did not therefore lose his religion. Enthusiasm is a term that in the estimation of Englishmen generally means a faulty excess.

[2] Hutton, in his admirable essay above quoted, talks as if Goethe had small capacity for friendship. But this is true only of a particular kind, of clinging and engrossing friendship which to some minds is a necessity. That Goethe did not require a friend, as some do, to look up to, was the necessary consequence of the Olympian character of his intellect. Jupiter on his throne may have many favourites, but no fellows.

[3] To the general charge of "moral indifference" brought against the great poet by Hutton and others, and to the assertion that he is altogether a stranger to the ideas of guilt, repentance, and remorse, I can in no wise subscribe. The poet's notion about a profitable *repentance* is expressed in

VII. The quick and ready susceptibility of which we have just spoken, might naturally have led —and has, in fact, not seldom led—poetic natures

the following lines from "Edwin and Elmira," one of his earliest productions:—

> " If it be noble in our hearts to keep
> The memory of our faults, and weigh them well,
> And in their room plant virtues, nevermore
> Can it be right and praiseful with long fret
> For past misdeeds to undermine the heart
> And lame the springs of action."

Here we have, in a few words, all that can justly be said about confession of sin, the burden of guilt, and repentance. There cannot be the slightest doubt that Goethe repented of his follies and misdeeds as honestly as other people do; and the poem from which these lines are translated, as well as his earliest production, "Die Launen der Verliebten," are a public confession of guilt—guilt in reference to the self-willed jealousy with which he tormented his first love, Katherine Schönkopf. So also, in the autobiography, he confesses not to have been without compunctions with regard to his conduct in giving up Frederika; and we can only admit so much of truth in the charge of habitual self-satisfaction brought against him, that he did not think it right to indulge largely in sorrow for past sins, because dwelling on the evils of the past, when the past cannot be remedied, can only serve to lame the hand for the present, and to dim the prospect for the future. "*Lass das Vergangene vergangen seyn*" is a maxim which he gives as a rule for a happy life, and which, when systematically acted on, leaves no room for prolonged exercises of sorrow for past misdeeds. It must be admitted, however, that the poet, in the second part of 'Faust,' not only wisely tempers, but seems altogether to overlook, the sorrow for sin that ought to have been felt into a sort of emotional dissipation and abandonment, which, if it does not end in vice and moral ruin, is certainly fatal to all true manhood. If it

and expressed by a sensualist of Faust's quality, before he was admitted into the fellowship of the "saints made perfect." No doubt repentance is best expressed by deeds, and that is what Goethe meant; but words have their rights, as in the expression of every human emotion, so specially under the sense of guilt. The deficiency of this expression in the second part of 'Faust,' and elsewhere, it may be, in the poet's works, is to be explained from two considerations: (1) the predominance of the æsthetical artistic above the moral in his intellectual constitution; (2) the length and breadth of his deep sympathy with humanity, which inclined rather to overlook or pity the moral aberrations of his fellow-sinners than to condemn them. That the painter and the preacher do not readily feel together; and that a predominant tendency to the one function tends to subordinate, and sometimes to misprize and to ignore the other, all experience teaches. The narrowness of the finite creature Man will in fact have it so. How large a segment of the complete circle of Goethe's heart the fine arts were, his life and writings emphatically declare. A striking example of this we have in the little poem on the great Diana of the Ephesians, in which his conservatism and his love of nature combine with his love of art to make him the apologist of the heathen goldsmith in his workshop, and to leave the fervid apostolic preacher outside in the cold. Again, if a large and catholic sympathy with humanity be, whether poetically or socially considered, one of the most enviable qualities of the human soul, like other virtues it has its limits, and when exerted beyond these limits necessarily becomes a vice. The virtue which this catholic sympathy begets, in its legitimate exercise, is toleration; the vice into which it grows, be the glory of a young man to flap his wings joyously and prove his strength, it is the business of a grown man to hold the reins tightly and to control by excess or misapplication, is indifference. With this moral indifference Goethe may sometimes seem chargeable; but fundamentally it is not so. His large human sympathy leads him to love the sinner, not to be indifferent to the sin. In the Venetian Epigrams, where a light and careless tone, sympathetic with low Italian life, prevails, he says :—

"*Greatest saints, we know, have been the most kindly to sinners: Here I'm a saint with the best; sinners I never could hate.*"

And this leads us directly to the main objection urged to the novel of the 'Elective Affinities,' that it makes vice attractive, and those who practise vice more interesting than the practisers of virtue. But here also we have a superficial judgment and a hasty conclusion. It is quite true that the two sinful parties in this novel are not represented as very repulsive personages; on the contrary, one of them, the lady, is drawn as a person of very remarkable sensibility and intelligence. But they are not represented as wise persons— rather as the slaves and victims of unreined emotions; and for this reason they are both hurried into ruin. The novel is a social tragedy of the deepest dye, of which the moral is the sanction of the civil bond of marriage—a bond so strong, that whosoever treats it lightly, even with the most plausible advocacy of sentiment, cannot escape the severest penalty. The amiable character of the offender only makes the tragic situation more intense, and the sanction of the moral law more imperative. The reader who does not see this moral in the novel is incapable of an æsthetical judgment: he condemns a part because he has not the range of thought to comprehend the whole. A similar objection was made to the 'Sorrows of Werther.' It was supposed to inculcate the suicide which it was written to condemn. Fervid passion the steeds. This essential feature of every admirable human character we find in Goethe strongly pronounced: however violently moved by passionate impulses from time to time, he never lost without the steady control of sober reason leads to ruin. This is the moral of 'Werther,' of the 'Elective Affinities,' as of our 'Hamlet.' In fact, in all tragedies the greatest sufferers are not represented as odious. Hamlet is not odious—noble rather; but he is not wise. The moral of the 'Elective Affinities' is far more plain than the moral of 'Hamlet.' Why, then, did people not see it? Simply because, as already remarked, they took offence at a small part, and forthwith condemned the whole. It was the old trick of hasty critics, which drew down the ridicule of Coleridge—viz., judging the sculpture by the blue spot in the marble. The spot, of course, had better not have been there; but the criticism was infinitely silly nothing the less. The only question is, why a wise man like Goethe should have deliberately chosen to insert an objectionable passage into his narrative, which was in no wise necessary to make an effective story? The simple answer to this is, that Goethe was too much of a pious worshipper of nature, in the sense of the best Greeks, to have been always sufficiently alive to the demands of certain delicate sensibilities, which have their root in the associations of the modern mind rather than in the absolute nature of things. This remark applies with equal force to the 'Roman elegies' and to certain passages of 'Wilhelm Meister.' With regard to these offences against good taste, we must simply say that the mind of the philosopher was not in perfect harmony with the feelings of a popular audience,—that he might have been to a certain extent touched with the low standard of the flat age in which he was born and bred,—two misfortunes, the one belonging to the individual, the other to the epoch, for which allowance will naturally be made by an equitable judge.

his balance; the equipoise of the soul became the watchword of his practical philosophy; and though the vessel of his fate, suddenly seized by the sweeping blast, might plunge and reel notably on occasions, the man at the helm was always there, with his head above the waves and his hand on the tiller. Self-control and self-mastery were as supreme in Goethe as in the breast of the sternest Stoic and the most severe Quietist. So much so, indeed, that those who have had no experience in themselves of this combination of moral contraries, in which all true greatness of character consists, have not been slow in Goethe's case to confound the cool control of manly reason with the cold and calculating selfishness of unsympathetic and unsocial minds. But to judge thus is to judge the oyster from the shell. The hardness of the external in this case does not exclude, but includes, the internal softness.

VIII. Poetical minds fall naturally under two great classes—those whose imagination is moved more powerfully by the sublime, and those who breathe more comfortably in the atmosphere of the beautiful. Of the former class Æschylus and Michel Angelo may be taken as types; of the latter, Sophocles and Raphael; and to this latter Goethe belongs. Of course the beautiful does not imply, according to Burke's unhappy confusion with the pretty, anything small — for the sea is beautiful shining in the sun, the sun is beautiful in its setting, and the flowers of the field and the leaves of the trees beautiful in their abundance. To Goethe the sight of any beautiful object was like delicate music to the ear of a cunning musician; he was carried away by it, and floated in its element joyously, as a swallow in the summer air, or a sea-mew on the buoyant wave. Hence the rich story of Goethe's loves, with which scandal, of course, and prudery, have made their market; but which, when looked into carefully, were just as much a part of his genius as Faust or Iphigenia, a part without which, indeed, neither Faust nor Iphigenia could possibly have been written. To a poet a beautiful woman always presents the most irresistible attraction: partly, no doubt, as with prosaic persons, because she is a woman and he a man, the one by nature plainly meant to be both the contrast and the complement of the other; partly also, and much more, because he is a poet, who both sees more sharply, and feels more keenly, and pictures more vividly the beauty of God's most beautiful piece of workmanship in the world of reasonable creatures. Let no man therefore take offence when I say roundly that Goethe was always falling in love, and that I consider this a great virtue in his character. Had he not done so, he would not have been half the man, nor the tenth part of the poet that he was. The only question here is, not how often he fell in love, for that is the part of accident, but how he comported himself when he did fall in love; for love, no doubt, like wine, is a thing that requires delicate handling, and, though essentially noble in its launch, if not well piloted, may often lead to most ignoble conclusions. The first notable love-affair of Goethe[1] was that universally known one with Frederika, the parson's daughter of Sesenheim, in the hill-country near Strasburg; and from which, it must be confessed, that Goethe, who was then a student preparing for his law degree at Strasburg, did not come off with an altogether clear reputation. Every English person has made up his mind—without much inquiry perhaps, but still very decidedly—that Goethe jilted this delightful young lady in a very shameful way; that he ought to have married her; and that he was well served for his ungentlemanly abandonment of so worthy a creature, by the less worthy specimen of her sex

[1] There was a prior one at Leipzig with Anna Katharina Schönkopf, his landlord's daughter, called *Kätchen*—but that was too juvenile an affair to call for serious consideration, and passed off quite innocently and happily for both parties. The lad was not in a condition to dream of marriage, and the girl had too much sense to wait for him.

into whose connubial toils he afterwards fell. I agree with this charge partly, but in no wise altogether. In endeavouring to pass a calm judgment on this capital charge—for the others are of minor significance—we must bear in mind that at the time of the entanglement the poet was a young man, a mere student—an undergraduate, as they say in Oxford—without any fixed profession or position. In this unripe state he fell in love with the parson's daughter, as only a Goethe or a Burns could fall in love, and the parson's daughter fell in love with him. This love went the length of kissing, and a tender correspondence of three months' duration; after which, as a thing of course, in the natural progress of such affairs marriage ought to have followed. And why did it not follow? simply because Goethe was a boy and not a man, and could not expect to get his parents' consent to the connection, or to make himself independent of that consent, unless he made up his mind to devote himself soul and body to the legal profession as a means of maintenance, which he would have looked upon as an act of intellectual suicide, and he was secretly determined not to do. We must bear in mind also that, though a boy in years, Goethe was a full-grown man in intellect; that, as we observed above, in his constitution extreme sensibility was coupled with an extraordinary power of cool survey; and however intensely he might love, he could never be such a slave to passion as not to know that hasty and ill-considered marriages of young persons without any firm footing in the world, have often been productive of an amount of misery through life, that far outweighed the pain of an early renunciation. We may observe, also, that every strong virtue in a man's character naturally, and sometimes necessarily, with the unavoidable change of circumstances, becomes a vice; and thus Goethe's extreme sensibility to his present environment, which was one of his greatest excellences, while it made him the most devoted of lovers in the presence of the fair one, necessarily exposed him to the charge of fickleness and variability when absent. A largely sympathetic nature will scarcely die of one lost love, while there is another quite near to supply its place. The man who during a long life can love only one woman, or live on one idea, is intense but narrow; like a sun, that should radiate only in one line, and, when that line fails, sinks into total night. Marriage under such circumstances and with such feelings was unadvisable; and he accordingly tore himself away with bleeding heart from the object of his affection. There was no fault, therefore, in breaking off the engagement, or rather in refraining to enter into an engagement which circumstances refused to recognise; the fault lay in the length of that very serious flirtation, to use a profane word, in which the poetical youth had allowed himself to indulge, and which he ought to have known could not be indulged in without inflicting a sore wound on an innocent female heart, not in any wise so readily curable as such wounds are in the rougher bosom of the male, and in the versatile susceptibility of a poetical temperament. So far, therefore, Goethe was guilty in this matter; and like an honest man, as he was, in his autobiography distinctly says so; but in a young man and a poet, and a first love-affair, a certain amount of guilt of this description is not so uncommon as that we should feel ourselves called upon studiously to intensify its hue and magnify its proportions. At all events, neither the unhappy lover himself, nor the good pastor's family, seemed to have looked upon the affair with the same severity of condemnation in which the English public has delighted to indulge; for, when the poet a few years afterwards revisited the scene of his first idyllic affection, he was received by the deserted object of his early love and her family in a fashion that indicated the silent sorrow rather than the moral indignation that had remained as the sting of the ill-starred adventure.[1]

[1] Had Goethe been guilty of the gross moral delinquency

Of the other loves of Goethe, that with Charlotte, the well-known heroine of 'Werther,' with Lili, and the Baroness von Stein, and Christiana Vulpius, who ultimately became his lawful wife, are the most famous,—the only ones, in fact, that require special notice, so far as a vindication of the poet's character in matters of the heart is concerned. His passion for Charlotte was an affair on which not even a shadow of slander can rest. Shortly after the young poet had transported himself for a season from Frankfurt to Wetzlar, in order to carry on, or seem to be carrying on, a superficial training in the subsidiary practice of the Imperial Chamber of Justice there, his fancy was charmed with the combination of natural sweetness, sprightliness, and domestic virtue manifested in the character of Charlotte Sophia Henrietta Buff, the golden-locked and blue-eyed daughter of Henry Adam Buff. But no sooner had the fine ecstasy of young love towards this fair creature begun to stir the nerves of the sensitive poet, than

in the matter of Frederika with which his severe English critics love to charge him, could he have written 'Clavigo' so shortly afterwards, or at all? The combined selfishness and cowardice of the principal character in this tragedy could scarcely have been portrayed in such vivid characters by a man who had deliberately been guilty of a similar baseness. Goethe's conduct in the Sesenheim affair was prudential; Clavigo's in the tragedy is treacherous.

he found out that the lady was engaged, or on the point of being engaged, to another—the Brunswick Councillor of Legation, John Christian Kestner, the father of the late Hanoverian minister in Rome. This discovery, of course, put an end to all thoughts of marriage; but the passion could not be so easily killed. Such a condition of things with a fiery lover, under a tropical sun, would infallibly have led to a stoppage of all intercourse, or to something very tragical or very bad. But the German nature is more kindly, more considerate, and more cool; so the intercourse of all the parties went on in this case as before—the bridegroom showing no jealousy, the bride a great amount of good sense, and the outside lover a great amount of self-command and strict repression of feelings that it would have been dishonourable to harbour. But Goethe was no Stoic; so he found it wisest at last to flee from the fascination, and give vent to the torture of an untenable position in a novel of sentiment. The next entanglement, with Lili, as she is called in the poet's lyrical works, was of an altogether different character; and though it contained nothing that could in the slightest degree be called dishonourable, was ineffective in its results, and called forth in its conduct certain traits of instability and unreliability in the character of the poet, for which he can scarcely hope to receive forgiveness, at least from the ladies. Anne Elizabeth Schönemann—the heroine of this second passion that, as in the case of Frederika, went to the point of marriage, but there halted—was the daughter of a rich Frankfurt banker, beautiful, accomplished, and extremely fascinating in her manner, and not without a slight touch of coquettish playfulness that only made her the more attractive. She belonged, also, to a society a little above the platform on which Goethe's family moved; and the brilliance of the fashionable saloon life, to which the young poet was for the first time introduced in her circle, might doubtless, as a novelty (for otherwise Goethe did not specially care for West-End manners), contribute to the power which she soon began to exercise over him. A mutual attachment soon revealed itself; and, as soon as revealed, the hindrance to a happy issue loomed in view. The parents on both sides were rather averse to the union: those of the lady because, in the fashion of the moneyed classes, they preferred to look up in the social scale for a son-in-law rather than down; those of the gentleman because, as Æschylus has it in the 'Prometheus,' unwise is the man who forms a connubial relation with a woman above his own rank in society. However, the disparity in this case was not so very great, and the opposition of the parents on both sides, by the intervention of a deft matchmaking lady, was so far overcome that it only required a stroke of decision on the part of the poet to drive a conclusive nail into the business. But the decisive stroke was not there. Why? The answer to this is not very clear,—as clearness, indeed, is not always easy in these matters, even to those who have the sharpest sight: but partly, we may conjecture, because the catholic fashion with which the bright, young, and fair one dispensed her charms may have excited emotions of mistrustful jealousy on the part of her imperious lover; partly because unfavourable reports of the catholic sensibilities of the gentleman may have reached the ears of the lady, with no weakened emphasis; partly because the parents of both parties, originally unfavourable, from whom an unwilling sort of assent seems to have been extorted, may have continued to send down a certain breath of indifference not favourable to decisive action; partly because in these matters delay gives time for consideration, which is fruitful in suggesting difficulties; partly because the lover in this case, though more now than a student, was not yet planted on such a firm stage of social independence as to enable him to encounter and to command the very perplexing and often disagreeable array of preparatory circumstances by which the narrow porch of real marriage is fenced off from the flowery field of ideal love;—but, whatever the secondary causes may have been that prevented the fair summer blossom of this love from bearing its natural fruit, the primary cause unquestionably was the want of decision and determination on the part of the lover. Another man of more passionate quality and more military directness of character could have made short work of all obstructions in such a state of matters, as easily as a boy walking through a corn-field would knock off the heads of the thistles with a stick. But God had made Goethe of different stuff. His power of self-survey and self-command was as remarkable as his extreme susceptibility. With such natures the passion of to-day readily turns over into the deliberation of to-morrow; and as it has been observed that a council of war never fights, so it may hold true that a council of love never marries. What turned the scale finally in the case of Lili was the appearance in Frankfurt of the Grand Duke of Weimar, a young prince, full of that fine, fresh, and frolicsome vitality which Goethe loved. The prince and the poet at once became brothers; and nothing would please the former but that the latter should follow him to his neat little Saxon capital, and assist him to enjoy life and to conduct business there. This offer Goethe willingly and wisely accepted; not, of course, because he cared particularly for courts, or had a hankering after titled personages, which was not at all in his nature, but rather because he was of an adventurous spirit, and was desirous above all things to escape from the small ways and cramping limitations that belonged to the life of a legal practitioner in Frankfurt. In the year 1775, when the destined hierarch of German literature was in his twenty-sixth year, he found himself settled for life in the, to him, altogether new scenes of the capital of one of the numerous tasteful little princedoms of the Fatherland; and with this new scene, new thoughts, new feelings, new enjoyments, and new duties crowded upon him, and overwhelmed him in such a masterful way, that the image of Lili, like that of Frederika, faded sweetly into the vague distance of the past; and marriage with the Frankfurt banker's daughter, or with any other woman, was for ten busy years, for reasons that we shall now proceed to describe, the last thing thought of by the rising young Jupiter of the Teutonic Olympus.

Before coming to Weimar, Goethe had received from a Hanoverian physician—Zimmermann, the author of the once widely read book on Solitude—an account of a lady of great beauty and greater accomplishments attached to the Court of Weimar. The admiration with which her portrait inspired him readily rose into a passion, when he looked on the fair reality face to face; for from that face there looked forth an eye of that rare quality "which sees everything as it is, and looks on everything with love"—an eye that could belong only to a woman in whose moral constitution was revealed that cunning combination of solid sense, high principle, and refined sentiment which is found in the most completely harmonised characters; and which was the ideal the young poet had all along been feeling after, and now at last seemed to have found.

The Baroness Charlotte von Stein was the wife of a respectable gentleman attached to the Court of the Grand Duke in the capacity of *Stallmeister*, master of the horse, groom of the archducal stables, or in whatever phrase the English version of the German title may delight. Goethe's previous loves were mere girls, on the sweet primrose-borderland between sixteen and seventeen. Charlotte von Stein was a woman past thirty years of age, fully six years older than the poet. She was a lady of high station, beautiful, gracious, talented, accomplished, womanly, sympathetic with the rising literature of Germany, a faithful wife, a good mother, a constant friend, and in every way attractive. This was the lady, a *beau idéal* of fully developed and finely harmonised chaste womanhood, whose potent graces were destined to pour a healing balm into the heart of Goethe, bleeding as it still was from the recently disturbed relations with Lili; and prepared by nature for the still nobler function of fostering and training the great representative genius of her country's literature, and affording to him a constant source of spiritual consolation in the trying circumstances of his early career at Weimar. For trying circumstances unquestionably they were to a man of his genius, to whom Court ceremonies and the details of official administration were only a little less disagreeable than the routine of a petty legal practice which he had left behind him at Frankfurt. During the whole weary ten years, of what the Germans call his Weimar apprenticeship, his beloved Charlotte, with whom he lived on the most intimate footing—in fact a sort of recognised member of the family—acted as a wise father-confessor to the poet; the one person in Weimar to whom he looked habitually as at once the inspirer of his purest inspirations, the chaste chastiser of his follies, the sweetener of his harshest labours, and the comforter of his sharpest sorrows. In the lives of few men has love—without which a true poet cannot live—taken such a noble form, and defied the power of such adverse circumstances to blast it; and perhaps it was precisely the very high strain with which this Platonic passion acted on the spiritual part of his nature, to the utter exclusion of other elements of his humanity, that, under altered circumstances, produced the reaction in a different direction, which it is now my duty to record.[1]

[1] Of course I am aware that the world generally, from its habitual want of charity in such matters, and Mr Lewes specially, in his Life of Goethe, has expressed himself very differently as to the nature of the relation between the passionate young poet and this celebrated Court beauty. But after a study of the published correspondence, and a consideration of the character of both the parties, and the nature of the circumstances, I see nothing to warrant the uncharitable judgment which may lightly be pronounced on this matter. The poet, with his extraordinary susceptibility to beauty and goodness in every shape, had, as we have seen on a previous occasion in the affair of Wetzlar, had the misfortune to be powerfully fascinated by the charms of a woman who was betrothed to another man; but he behaved on this occasion with the most perfect honour, never attempted to conceal his admiration from the destined husband, and when he found that he could stand the disturbing fascination no longer, took safety in flight. A similar temptation from Brentano's wife he resisted in the same manly way (Duenzer, p. 202). But retreat in this shape was not possible at Weimar; once attached to the Court there, the high-strung young poet and the high-toned lady in whom he had at last found his ideal of womanhood were condemned to see one another every day. What was to be done? Of course a poet, to whom the worship of his ideal is a moral necessity, could not cease to love; and the lady would have been more than human had she remained persistently insensible to the worship paid to her by such a man, and to the inspiring and elevating influence of intellectual communion with him. Like not a few

That a man in the full vigour of manhood, full of fervid passion, and in all respects, physical, intellectual, and moral, perhaps the most complete man that the recent centuries have set their eyes on, should have remained unmarried till an age closely bordering on forty—ten years more than the *mezzo cammin di nostra vita* of which Dante speaks—is a phenomenon not exactly belonging to the normal state of things, and, in

wives of fine intellectual sensibilities, she had an appetite for spiritual nourishment, which her husband, a commonplace man of business, could do nothing to gratify. She therefore made up her mind, securely cased in her own virtue, and with the full privacy of her husband, to admit the fascinating stranger into her family circle on the most intimate terms, and to be his bosom friend and confidential adviser in all that was most dear to his heart. Every woman could not have done this; but let the uncharitable world for once believe that Charlotte von Stein was an exceptionally good woman, as Goethe was, I am firmly convinced, an exceptionally good man. No man had a more profound respect for the sacredness of the marriage-tie; and it is in no wise probable that a writer who wrote a novel with the acknowledged moral of the famous text, Matthew v. 28 (see this volume, p. 125), would have passed ten years of his life in direct contravention of it. I may add that Mr Hutton, in the little that he says about the connection with the Baroness von Stein, hits the key-note in this case equally becoming to a judicious biographer and a good Christian. "There is no need to judge the matter at all," says he. "It is almost the only case in which Mr Lewes paints another in dark colours, without justification, for his hero's sake."—Essays, ii. 70.

Goethe's case, only to be explained by the powerful charm which the accomplished Baroness exercised over him. So long as the poet lived in Weimar, under the somewhat oppressive and repressive action of Court life and administrative duty which overlaid him there, and so long as such a superior woman as this his second Charlotte was present with the daily balm of her chaste love to pour into his wounds, marriage was out of the question. But the permanence of this delicate relation depended, as in the case of everything human, to a certain extent on the permanence of the circumstances out of which it arose; and so, when Goethe, to shake off for a season the burden of secular affairs, which had encroached largely on his poetical activity during the ten years of his first Weimar service, at length obtained leave to plunge into the sea of sunny nature and artistic grace, for which he had long sighed, in Italy, it could not be otherwise than that a new and more lusty life should well up within him, which made him more independent of the soothing balm poured into his soul from his fair confessor. After nearly two years of voluptuous communion with nature and stimulant study of art in Rome, and other centres of refined attraction and rich historical association in the land to which all ideal passion naturally gravitates, Goethe returned to

Weimar a wider, a broader, and a stronger man, and a man certainly over whom a single woman, even a woman of such high character and rare accomplishment as Charlotte von Stein, could not hope to exercise such an exclusive sovereignty as had long been conceded to her, or, to speak more accurately, rather forced upon her by the poet. The consequence was, on their meeting again, a marked coolness compared with the fervour which had glowed at their parting; a sensible loosening of the bonds which once held them together as strong as adamant; and then an open expression of dissatisfaction on the part of the lady, to which Goethe could make no satisfactory reply. He wished, no doubt, the old relation to continue; but he was too honest to say that it could continue under the same condition of absolute dependence. He was in every way a more happy and a more life-enjoying mortal than he had been, when he left the object of his Platonic affection. He might say nothing: but women are quick to observe, and, like Churchmen, fond of power; and the lady in this case had been too long accustomed to an unqualified sovereignty over the greatest intellect and the biggest heart of the time to be willing to hold the reins of his affection with a less absolute sway. What happened may readily be divined. Emancipated, partly by a biennial absence, and partly by the unconcealed coolness, and, as Goethe thought, unmerited reproach on the part of his Platonic love, the tendency towards a non-Platonic attachment, such as common mortals practise, and many look upon as the only legitimate kind of love, resumed its natural sway: and so one pleasant morning, when the poet was in a happy humour, taking a walk in the Park at Weimar, there tripped up to him "a pretty little blond lassie, with beautiful blue eyes, swelling lips, and a full round face, a neat little nose, and long golden locks," with a petition in her hand in behalf of her poor brother, which she presented to the great man in the most graceful way. Goethe, with his usual kindness, ever ready to help a fellow-mortal in distress, used his influence successfully to get the brother the desired promotion; and as an addition to this service, the pretty little sister, to her own great surprise, found the biggest man in Weimar next to the Grand Duke, and the greatest genius in Germany, had actually fallen in love with her innocent little ways, and determined to make her his wife. To this she had no objection; though, perhaps, if she had possessed a little more self-esteem and been of higher pretensions, she might have seen good occasion to pause; for the poet, whether it was that he wished to do the thing on the spot, beyond the reach of Weimar tattle and the objections of parties who would insist on interfering where they had no business,[1] or whether from a dislike to ecclesiastical ceremonies in matrimonial matters, or because being fresh from Italy and full of polytheistic notions, he was not in the humour of having his human passion consecrated by the customary Christian rites—by whatever serious reason moved or light whim, certain it is that he suddenly showed himself to the polite Weimar Court and Weimar world as a married man, without the recognised stamp of respectability on the bond, bound only by the tie of what the Germans call a *Gewissens Ehe*, a marriage of conscience; that is, he treated Christiana Vulpius as his married wife from that time forward, and enjoyed all the fulness of domestic happiness with her for many years, which common mortals enjoy with their legitimately conjugated yoke-fellows. Of course after this the close connection with the Baroness von Stein ceased; Goethe might have been quite willing to let her still retain the higher half of himself, to which Christiana could put forth no claims; and, had the poet been only a little more guarded in his previous expressions of absolute devotion to his fair confessor, there was no reason why the old Platonic connection should be broken off

---

[1] A Gaelic proverb says: "If you wish to be blamed, marry; if you wish to be praised, die!"

by a marriage in the style of common mortals, in which, as the chaste wife of another, the lady could have no part; but the stroke was too sudden, and the wrench too cruel—the declension also from herself, a highly accomplished German Court lady, to what in Scotch song is called "a bonnie lassie," seemed as unworthy of the poet as it was unpleasant to herself: and years were required to harden the surface of a wound, which a passing touch, in its crude freshness, would cause to bleed. But this was not all: the Weimar public and the German people had good reason to feel displeased with the poet; not, indeed, for taking to wife, as many were forward to say, a woman of inferior station to himself and the Court ladies with whom he habitually associated — but for the public violation of those external proprieties in connubial ceremonial, which, as human beings are constituted, unquestionably have both a human value and a divine right in society, and which a wise man of forty years of age, well versed in the ways of the world, and not in general given to despise social conventions and traditional usages, should not have allowed himself to defy. In this view of the matter the public were undoubtedly right; beyond that, whatever has been said either in Germany or England with regard to this union appears to me altogether unwarranted. A great poet, like any other man, has a right to choose a wife after his own fancy; and if he either chooses the wrong woman, or marries her, as in this case, in the wrong way, it is only another proof how Nature has determined to keep the reins of love strongly in her own hands, and to make the wisest feel that once in their life at least she can make them do a foolish thing.[1]

[1] "Goethe was not ignorant that his union with Christiana had placed him in a false position to society; as little could he conceal from himself the fact that, however engaging and lovable she might be in many ways, she could not offer him that communion of souls which it was his nature to seek, and which was no less necessary in order to surround his family with those influences which could proceed only from a more highly gifted mother; but his true love to her, and his noble character, prevented him from ever thinking of a divorce; on the contrary, he afterwards saw the propriety of elevating her, by the ceremonial stamp of the Church, up to the platform of matrimonial respectability required by the customs of society" (Dünzer, 'Leben Goethe,' p. 511); which means that the union with Christiana was a mistake and a folly, which the poet turned into a virtue as far as was in his power. From the whole affair, those who choose may draw the moral—*Alles rächt sich auf Erden.* Had he married Frederika, this folly and this mistake would certainly have been prevented. So Schutz Wilson, in an interesting paper, "The Loves of Goethe," in 'Studies and Romances'—London, 1873. Lewes, in his 'Life of Goethe,' vol. ii. ch. viii., has spoken very nobly and very justly in defence of Christiana. Hutton, pp. 37-91, also speaks in a very kindly way about her; at the same time, however, in my opinion, con-

IX. These remarks on the love-affairs of the great German poet have been drawn out to a length considerably out of proportion to the general

demning Goethe in much stronger terms than either a just philosophy or a large charity seems to allow.

There is one circumstance connected with Christiana Vulpius which, as it goes closely into the inmost recesses of the poet's personal character, can scarcely be omitted here. She is the heroine of the celebrated 'Roman Elegies,' which form the main point of offence in the moral aspect of Goethe's genius as a great national poet. It was an offence in Germany to many of the poet's greatest admirers, when it came out; it is an offence in England much more, though, for obvious reasons, not so much spoken about as the affair of Frederika. We must therefore endeavour, with all impartiality, to make a special appraisement of it, and for this purpose shall state the case fairly on both sides. First, from the point of view of the general public, the case would naturally be stated thus: These 'Roman Elegies' are merely a transplantation of the æsthetico-sensual love-poetry of the Romans into modern European soil. This was both artistically a blunder and morally a fault: a blunder in art, because it bears on the face of it the character of an echo and an imitation; a fault in morals, because to represent the noblest passion of the human mind under one of its lowest aspects, must be a fault in a lyric poet who breathes a lofty atmosphere, from which that type can derive no nourishment. More than this, the representation of love, under what is mainly a sensuous aspect, by a man of influential genius, cannot be without a baleful influence in the field of practical morals, stimulating passions which are by nature sufficiently strong, and throwing a gloss of poetical sentiment over a course of sensual indulgence which philosophy and religion equally condemn. To this the poet, from his point of view, would naturally reply:

scheme of this paper, not so much from their intrinsic importance in the moral contents of Goethe's life, as from the great amount of gossip and scandal

Nature, not convention, has always been the goddess that I worship. I find in Nature the sensuous man and the spiritual man; and in my profession as a poet or interpreter of Nature, I pay respect to both. It was always a necessity with me, whatever experience I went through in life, the great teacher, to represent that experience under its poetical aspect; for everything in nature has its poetical aspect, and that aspect I am bound to find out and to express. Now, with regard to my 'Roman Elegies,' what are the facts of the case? Italy and art had been my dream from my youth; but from the realisation of that dream I had been debarred by a long service of disagreeable, and to me, as a poet, unprofitable public duty in Weimar. Escaped at length from these bonds, I found myself in the sunny land of natural and artistic beauty, my own master at last, and free to lay myself open to all the gracious influences, historical and æsthetical, which flow in upon every receptive soul there. Is it a wonder or a matter of regret that the genius of the three great triumvirs of love, Ovid, Tibullus, and Propertius, should have acted powerfully on me there? Love was always the most powerful instinct in my soul, and the present environment, whatever it might be, was not less powerful. I count it no shame to have been guilty of this sort of imitation, as we all borrow from one another: when in Rome I borrowed from Rome and schemed my 'Elegies,' as in Weimar I schemed my 'Tasso' from the influences of Court life which worked upon me there. But this is not all. My 'Roman Elegies,' though their scenery was furnished by Rome, were not written in Rome, nor was any Roman girl the heroine of my Propertian loves. The 'Elegies' were written in Thuringia, after my return from Italy; and the heroine of the 'Elegies' that is apt to gather round such matters, and from the manifest difficulty of making a true statement of such cases without entering into personal

was my excellent wife, Christiana Vulpius, with whom I have lived in domestic peace, as the happy father of a happy family, for thirty years. That sweetest solace of my Weimar life I met with shortly after my return from Italy. The time and the woman suited; and so I made a Roman girl of her, that she might live in my memory, and go down to posterity, indissolubly intertwined with the happiest days of my life, and the most significant spot in the records of the human race. So much might the poet say for himself in this matter, and certainly not without effect; the most important point in the defence being that he did not, as Lord Byron in Venice, live a life of loose sensuality in Rome, but that the love-scenes at bottom are merely a glorification of his wife. We will add a further plea in palliation. If it be certain, as we have good reason to believe, that Goethe was not at any period of his life a licentious man, and that his connection with the Baroness von Stein was of a purely Platonic character, then the restraint thus put upon the physical part of his nature for so long a period, through the bloom of youth and the vigour of manhood, avenged itself by a natural plunge into the opposite, in the indulgence of a love equally human, though not so elevating. All this, however, has only the air of an apology; and though, to adopt legal phraseology, the strongest charges in the indictment must be departed from, it seems impossible to acquit the poet altogether, either of the æsthetical blunder or the moral fault. Our verdict might stand thus: The double nature of man is undeniable, and the complete man and the great poet must contain and acknowledge both; but the relationship which exists between them is not that of equality but of subordination; the relation not of the two kings of Sparta or the two Roman consuls, but details. Those who feel inclined to pass a severe judgment on our German wise man because of his extreme sensibility to female beauty, ought further

of master and man, of rider and horse—a relation so close that the inferior may never be allowed to assert itself independently, but must be content to appear as the natural vassal of the superior. No doubt in dramatic poetry the low and the high elements that constitute humanity may be embodied separately in deficient or corrupt characters; but the æsthetical and moral effect of a drama depends on the tone, drift, and upshot of the whole concatenation of characters and incidents; whereas in lyric poetry the impression is made by one person, one passion, and one situation, which, if they are on a low platform of sentiment and conception, stamp the whole work as of a low order. Herein, if we are not mistaken, lies the error of Goethe in the 'Elegies'; he transposed the æsthetical rights of the drama into lyrical poetry, and thereby sinned against the rights of the moral nature, which in all art, as in everything human, must be supremely respected. Goethe's mind was essentially dramatic, or objective, as the Germans call it, and no doubt beneficially so, for his lyrics, as well as for dramas strictly so called; but still in lyric poetry the subjective emotion must dominate, and the dominating emotion must be of the ennobling and elevating character which belongs to all true poetry. Now what have we in the 'Roman Elegies'? The original of the heroine, we are assured, was Goethe's wife: but she does not appear as a wife or a bride, like the fair one in the Song of Solomon; she is merely a pretty Roman girl, lightly picked up in a Roman *osteria*, and with no attractions beyond what would have made her an agreeable companion of luxurious hours to an Ovid or a Propertius, breathing the impure atmosphere of decadent Romanism under Augustus. It may be urged in defence of this style of portraying connubial bliss that Titian has to bear in mind also, that there is perhaps not one among the great leaders of thought in the history of the world the details of whose life lie so syste-

painted many naked beauties in the Greek style, which the walls of polite saloons, and even Episcopal palaces, do not disdain to receive as a fitting decoration. But the lines which separate the sister domains of poetry and painting, appear nowhere so distinctly as in this example. Painting has to do with form and colour alone, and therefore must make the most of them; poetry has the free range of human thought, passion, and action, and will not be readily allowed to expatiate in a field which is only the smallest part of its vast domain. And here we seem to have touched a point of weakness in Goethe as a poet, which comes out elsewhere, specially in the second part of 'Faust.' He allows the painter's brush to usurp the province of the poet's pen; and instead of a noble passion presents us with a graceful picture. And thus it may appear that his assiduous practice of the arts of design, while it improved his poetry in one direction, damaged it in another; so difficult is it for the most richly equipped human being to divide his faculty, and to do more than one great thing greatly. But a more serious charge remains. The immoral influence of Titian's beauties is likely null; the finest works of art serve no higher purpose with the mass of men than to entertain the eye for a passing moment; but the great poet, though not a preacher, is a teacher and a trainer, and men look to him for guidance and direction through life. Now the passion of love is one which, above all others, it must be the business of a great poet to elevate and to purify; for from no passion, not even the lust of drinking and gambling, do more evil issues flow to society, and deeper degradation, than from this imperious instinct of love, when its animal constituent is unnaturally separated from the spiritual. On the face of them the 'Romatically bare before his critical fellow-men. Did we know the private life of Sophocles, Chaucer, Shakespeare, and others of our *Dii majorum gentium*

man Elegies' deal with this nobler passion, if in an extremely graceful, certainly in a rather slippery fashion; and this is a fault of which a great and a good man like Goethe ought not to have been guilty; a wise man also, and one who was bound to consider not only the innocency of his poetical portraiture, so far as himself was concerned, but the impression which it might make on the multitudinous young readers into whose hands the books of a great national poet naturally fall. The apology which he made, when charged with these most natural objections to his erotic compositions, shows only the more strongly the great mistake he had committed in their composition. In a poetical epistle to an esteemed friend, who had spoken to him seriously on this point, he replies, in the first place, that books are of little consequence in the world; the character of young persons is formed, not by anything that poets may write, but by everything that a living man does.

"*Es bildet
Nur das Leben den Mann, und wenig bedenten die Worte.*"

And again, when his friend makes special reference to the young ladies of the family—

"*Die mir der kuppelnde Dichter mit allem Bösen bekannt macht*"—

he says that the young ladies are very nice creatures, and find plenty to do in the kitchen, the laundry, the nursery, the cellar, and the garden, without reading books. If they have any idle time on their hands occasionally, they will naturally ask for a cookery-book; and, so far as he himself is concerned, had he had a dozen daughters in his house, he in the world of books, there might be blue spots there also in the marble, on which calumny would eagerly fix, and scandal would delight to gloat. Even the most sober pilot is not at all times equally master of the helm. What remains of this panoramic glance at a great human life admits of being stated more concisely. And, in the first place, in no view does the great manhood of Goethe's character show more effectively than in the ten years of his early Weimar apprenticeship, to which we have already alluded. From the high trust reposed in his diligence and fidelity by the Grand Duke, he soon found himself in the very difficult position of being both head and hand in the various departments of the civil administration of the principality. Goethe was not the man either to act ungratefully

---

would find them enough to do, without sending more than once in the year to the circulating library! This is very lame, and we may add, very German and very Greek; the English young ladies certainly will never altogether forgive the man who wrote thus, though no doubt they are generally preserved by very wise advice, as well as by a very healthy instinct, from reading anything that might do them harm. But what shall we say to the young gentlemen? If they should be found in Roman vineyards or *osterias*, practising Propertian loves loosely (as Byron did in Venice), with the 'Roman Elegies' in their pocket, would the spirit of the man who wrote 'Iphigenia' and 'Tasso,' or the author of all those wise discourses in 'Eckermann,' look down with complacency upon that?

to the patron who had so graciously advanced him, or to perform in a perfunctory fashion any work, however troublesome, that Providence threw in his way. Whatever he did, he did with all earnestness and with all thoroughness,—and that is the condition of all profitable work in this world, whether inspired by genius or directed by talent. The mines, the universities, the finances, the Church patronage, the Court ceremonials, and, not least, the management of the theatre,—all gradually slipt into the hands of the new untitled man from shopkeeping Frankfurt; not, of course, without notable grudge and envy at first from the troop of hereditary expectants of place and promotion whom he supplanted. But in the end talent and character triumphed gloriously over all these obstructions; and not, as in the case of our Disraeli, because the young literary adventurer had determined by imperious volition to make himself a great politician, but because, without any express intention of meddling with matters of administration, or having any special pleasure in them, the poet had grandly made up his mind to adapt himself to the circumstances into which he had been thrown, and make the best of them. A talent for business is the exception with literary men of all descriptions, and particularly with poets. But, though Goethe at an early period of life had secretly resolved to escape from the barren subtleties and bloodless abstractions of the law, he had sense enough to know that the root of all healthy literature is to be found only in a large experience of life, and that a complete and well-rounded manhood, manifested in a wisely guided and prosperous social career, could not be achieved by a one-sided culture of the emotional and imaginative faculties; in other words, if his destiny, as he dimly divined, was to be a great German poet, he must first make himself an effective German man. This was the consideration unquestionably that led him to remain at Weimar, squandering, as might appear to many, his brilliant talents in getting up Court shows and masquerades, and ministering in other shapes to the pleasures of his princely patron. It may be very true that his position as a leading courtier in a petty German principality was not the most favourable to the growth of a robust poetical talent. No doubt the atmosphere which Æschylus breathed at Athens, with sword in hand, amid the great Persian wars, and our Shakespeare at London, in the stirring era of good Queen Bess, was much more invigorating. It could not possibly be advantageous for a man of large calibre and comprehensive survey to live the centre of a small circle of admiring worshippers. All this no man knew better than the poet himself; but it was not in his power either to make a new situation for himself, or to disown the duties which his position plainly imposed upon him. Every man, he justly considered, must go through a certain routine of uncongenial hard work, in order to acquire for himself a stage on which his geniality may disport itself with dignity and ease; and most of all the poet,—" a wingèd animal," as Plato calls him—though with his wings he soars into the fellowship of the gods,—must bear in mind that he writes poetry not for gods, but for men; and that he cannot hope, whether for their pleasure or their profit, largely to move those from whose habitation he dwells remote, and with whose pursuits he will not condescend to sympathise. It is possible to spoil poetry,—at least, to make it practically unprofitable to the great majority of men,—by being too poetical.

X. If Goethe was an office-bearer and a courtier, and finally a Prime Minister and a titled dignitary, in a German principality at the time of the great French wars, he could not avoid being in some sense a politician; and the part which he played, or rather did not play, in the great social upheavals and overturnings symbolised by the name of the great Napoleon, has exposed him to no very measured criticism on the part of the political enthusiasts of the hour.[1] But Goethe, like Plato, was by constitution the representative of order and authority; and it was as unreasonable to blame him for not sympathising with the social volcanoes, earthquakes, and thunderstorms of the great revolutionary period, as to have blamed Erasmus for not being Martin Luther, or Wordsworth for not being Percy Bysshe Shelley. The political type to which strong characters like Goethe and Byron belong is marked out from their cradle; the one a born Conservative of the stable type, the other a born Liberal of the mobile type—and both belonging as essentially to the divinely constituted antagonism of things as the bones and the blood to the physical structure of the body. Give me a well-defined sphere, however narrow, which I can command, said Goethe, and create order out of chaos: Give me liberty, said Byron, to pluck the beard of all authority, and acknowledge no restraints, human or divine; and the big world is not big enough for me. And as for patriotism, Goethe's patriotism consisted in doing the work of administration well where God had intrusted him with such work; and he believed that for the great purposes of government one wise and strong man at the helm of state is better than the congregated babblement of a hundred fools. Fervid patriots at the

[1] For this country see the Edinburgh Review for July 1857.

era of the great Liberation war never forgave him for having, in what they thought a servile and cowardly manner, done homage to the genius of the great Napoleon; but they forgot that the poet, as a philosopher and a man of a cosmopolitan mind, could not cherish in his large heart the bitter animosities and the irreconcilable hatreds which belong to patriotism in men of narrow sympathies, and in times of feverish excitment. Goethe was no partisan of Napoleon; but his habitual tone of impartial survey led him rather to admire the great man than to hate the strong Frenchman. It was not in his nature to hate anybody, much less wholesale to denounce a people to whom Europe owes so much of its highest culture and most winning grace as to the French. These Teutonic " French-eaters" forgot also that Phocion, one of the most virtuous of Athenian citizens, performed the same part, or, to be more precise, a much more positively and energetically unpatriotic part, in reference to the then dominant Macedonian dynasty; they forgot, also, that Goethe was sixty years old when this flaming sympathy for the restoration of the great German empire of Charlemagne was expected to spring, like Minerva, full-grown out of his brain. If a Körner, and an Arndt, and a Stein, and a Schenkendorf were required at that time to pave the way for a Bismarck, who, two generations afterwards, by happy blunders from without, and drastic treatment with blood and iron from within, should realise the dreams of the soldiers of the Liberation war,—the sexagenarian poet Goethe could no more be expected to play the part of that Arndt, or of that Stein, than Plato could have been expected to play the part of Demosthenes had he drawn out his years to the brink of the fatal battle of Chæronea. Who ever blamed Gioberti for not being a republican like Mazzini, or Walter Scott for not being a reformer like Henry Brougham?

XI. Not less wonderful, in my opinion much more wonderful, than his active part in official life at Weimar, was the warm interest which he there took in all the sciences most closely connected with the sphere of his public duty. These were mineralogy, geology, botany, and anatomy; in all which he took not only an interest, such as a superficial observant and sympathetic poet would naturally take; but, as in everything else, so in science, he took a firm grip of whatever came near him, and, as specially in the case of botany and osteology, cast a prophetic glance of divination into one of the inner mysteries of the framework of natural science, which obtained slow but sure recognition from the great masters in those departments. What we admire here is not only the union of scientific analysis with imaginative construction, so rare amongst men of poetical genius, but the stout purpose and systematic persistency with which the poet from time to time, in the midst of his poetical creations, carried on the large inductions necessary for the verification of what he had so felicitously divined. And if, in another branch of natural science—viz., OPTICS—from an ignorance or misprision of mathematics, for which he had no organ, he was led into the conceit of an imaginary discovery, in respect of which his customary sagacity seems to have deserted him, we can only say here, that *non omnia possumus omnes*, and the aberrations of great men are often more instructive than the right lines of the small.[1]

XII. A philosopher, in the professional sense of the word, and in the prominent attitude of his mind, like Plato in Athens, Spinoza in Holland, or Leibnitz in Hanover, Goethe was not; but no one who has either read his life or studied his 'Faust,' can fail to perceive that in respect of a native genius

---

[1] Those who are specially interested in the scientific studies of the poet may consult the German work quoted in my Preface, and, with regard to Optics, read an excellent discourse on Goethe's 'Farbenlehre' by Professor Tyndall, Royal Institution, March 19, 1880.

for dealing with principles, and of an actual working his way through metaphysical difficulties, he was a philosopher, and as such a fitting representative of that nation in modern times which has most completely reproduced the speculative subtlety for which the ancient Greeks were so famous. "*Alle philosophie,*" said he, with his usual penetrating realism, "*muss geliebt und gelebt werden;*" and so much of it as a great poet required to live and love through he had unquestionably lived and loved. Let him be compared in this regard with Scott, or Burns, or Byron, and we shall see how distinctly, perhaps in some respects disadvantageously for his poetry, he is a philosopher; and as characteristically as Plato represented both the æsthetical and the metaphysical elements of his country in being pre-eminently the poetical philosopher, no less characteristically did the author of 'Faust' perform the like function to his people in being the philosophical poet.[1]

XIII. Closely connected with philosophy, indeed only another name for it in its higher departments,

[1] Schiller, who evidently made a profound study of Goethe's intellect, says: "Your peculiar way of alternating between reflection and production is truly enviable and admirable. Both species of activity are wholly distinct in you; and this is precisely the reason why both are so well developed."— Briefe, 2d Jan. 1798.

is theology. In this science, as in all matters of deep human concern, Goethe took through life the liveliest interest. While on the one hand he had enough of the sceptic in his constitution to prevent him from building upon any rash dogmatism; on the other hand, the fine equipoise of his character kept him quite free from the fashionable vice of certain physical scientists in England at the present moment, the vice of denying God altogether, that they may escape from the suspicion of being tainted with any of the vulgar errors and philosophical misconceptions that in popular parlance, or scholastic schematism, are identified with the use of the sacred name. He believed firmly in God, in a moral government of the world, and in a future life. To everything else in religion, whether orthodoxies or heterodoxies, he was alike indifferent. He accepted the Bible in its main substance and drift as God's most significant revelation of Himself in the moral world, just as in the works of Greek art he had revealed his perfections in the domain of the beautiful; but he would hear nothing of that separation of God from nature, which with a certain severe class of dogmatic theologians, as with the whole school of ascetics and devotees, had been paraded as the most perfect form of religion. Rather with him, as with the poet Coleridge and the Apostle James, true

religion consisted in the love and reverence of
everything good and truly beautiful, and in
keeping himself unspotted from the arbitrary
conventions, unfruitful opinions, and absurd customs of the world. " He prayeth best who
loveth best;" and he worships God most worthily who is most eager to forward God's purpose
in his own sphere of work, and to strengthen
his fellow-labourers in theirs. WORK, indeed, always with love and never with hatred, was his
grand text, rule, and shibboleth; and whoso
worked not thus was a *dilettante*, a cumberer of
the ground, and the sooner he was rooted out the
better. For the general charge of SELFISHNESS
brought against him in such sweeping terms by
English people, I have not been able to find the
slightest ground. Never ready to take offence,
never harbouring a grudge, ever willing to help
where his help could be useful, in every relation
he was not only a great and a noticeable, but
a good, pleasant, brotherly, kindly, human, and
thoroughly enjoyable man.

XIV. One accomplishment of the poet cannot
be passed over in silence. He was by early and
special instinct a draughtsman as well as a poet;
and this is the more remarkable, as very few men
of the highest excellence in poetry have been able

or willing to bestow any large share of their attention on the sister arts of design. But the great German, with his polypus-like forth-putting of feelers, exercised himself in this province so assiduously and so continuously, that it may seem doubtful whether this close training of the eye on the beauties of form and colour did not damage him in the domain of eventful action and discursive passion, which more peculiarly belongs to the poet; but, however this may be, it is on the other hand certain that an eye well exercised in the details of art will never allow itself to float about in that region of transcendental mistiness, overstrained fancifulness, and gorgeous unreality of all kinds, in which some notable poets in these latter days seem to have thought it a special sign of genius to indulge.

XV. Lastly, Matthew Arnold somewhere has characterised Goethe as "the greatest poet of the present age, and the greatest critic of all ages." This dictum is perhaps very near the truth in both limbs, and specially in the latter. It is not generally expected that a great poet should be a great critic. Inspiration is apt to smother rather than to foster judgment. "Contented to enjoy what others understand" may well have been the true expression for the intellectual attitude of a Shakespeare, a Tasso, and a Thorwaldsen, and many of the biggest names in the world of constructive art; but in certain richly compounded natures, such as Plato, Scott, and Goethe, we may see plainly that the faculty of just survey and catholic appreciation has coexisted along with exquisite sensibility and fervid passion; the prophet is master of his inspiration, if not always in the moment of possession, certainly by a sure reaction after the fit is over; and, as in Goethe's case particularly, where a man has lived an active literary life on a broad European stage to the ripe age of seventy or eighty, he can scarcely fail to have grown up into a ripeness of sound judgment in æsthetical matters analogous to that finely trained instinct which guides the decisions of great jurists on the bench. Add to this, that the large appetite for intellectual appropriation, which we noted above as one of the leading characteristics of the poet's intellect, accompanied him to his latest years; and we shall readily understand how no star of any magnitude, whether it were a Béranger in France or a Manzoni in Italy, a Byron in England or a Burns in Scotland, could appear on the literary horizon of Europe without receiving from the sage old Aristarchus of Weimar a careful study and a loving appreciation.

XVI. It was no part of the scheme of these

remarks to give a critical appreciation of Goethe's literary productions. His character and completeness as a man personally and socially, is what I have aimed at indicating in its salient features. The high position which he holds as the great representative literary man of Germany, though not so popular with certain classes as Schiller, may be assumed as certified by the general assent of Europe.[1] His name is as potent a court of appeal

[1] It may be worth while here to append Mr Hayward's verdict, as perhaps the last well-qualified writer who has spoken authoritatively on the literary reputation of the poet:—

"Although nearly half a century has elapsed since Goethe's death, his reputation, constantly on the increase, stands higher, and on a more solid foundation, at the present moment, than at any preceding period. No dissent was provoked by the lecturer who, addressing a cultivated Berlin audience, recently compared his influence on the spiritual atmosphere of Germany to that of a convulsion of the heart, which should raise the climate many degrees in warmth, enrich vegetation, improve the whole aspect of the land, and supply a new base of life. Nor has that influence been confined to Germany. Distinct signs of it have been recognised in the spiritual atmosphere of England, where, besides more temperate admirers, there exists a respectable school who swear by him. 'The voices for Goethe,' says Mr Carlyle, 'compared with those against him, are in the proportion, as we reckon them, both as to number and value, of perhaps a hundred to one. We take in, not Germany alone, but France and Italy—not the Schlegels and Schellings, but the Manzonis and De Staëls.' . . . Except 'Faust,' there is no other work of Goethe which can be called first-rate of its

in this nineteenth century as Voltaire's was in the eighteenth ; and as superior to the brilliant Frenchman in all the highest moral and intellectual qualities, as the age and the people to which he belonged was more earnest, more positive, and more reverential. One leading characteristic only of his literary workmanship, intimately connected as it is with his character, it may not seem inappropriate to specify in conclusion. It is this: with Goethe the ideal and the real were always identical, the one growing by a natural necessity from the root of the other, and developing itself, after the analogy of the flowery world, into blossom and fruitage, by a beautiful process of metamorphosis. So it was, no doubt, fundamentally with Homer, and Shakespeare, and Scott, and Burns, and with all first-

kind; but take them all together, and where shall we find a richer cluster, a brighter constellation, of poetry, romance, science, art, philosophy, and thought? 'Goethe,' observes Madame de Staël, 'should not be criticised as an author good in one kind of composition and bad in another. He rather resembles nature, which produces all and *of* all ; and we can prefer in him his climate of the south to his climate of the north, without disregarding in him the talents which harmonise with these different regions of the soul.' In whichever of these regions we encounter him, we recognise a master-mind; and without pretending to fix his precise place amongst the greatest poets, we do not hesitate to declare him the most splendid specimen of cultivated intellect ever manifested to the world."

class poets; but the process in Goethe's case was more thoroughly worked out, or, at all events, can be traced biographically with more instructive minuteness. To submit himself freely and unreservedly to the action of all natural influences and social facts—to lose himself, so to speak, in his surroundings, and then to retire into himself and carry about with him, and reproduce in suitable form whatever of great or beautiful impressions they had communicated—was the problem of his life and the secret of his craft. Therefore his poems, however light and airy in appearance, have a firm root of reality in them, which makes them as humanly true in their sphere as the solid and flesh-like portraits of Titian and Rembrandt; he never has more wings than bones, or more sail than ballast. His lyrics are never pretty soap-bubbles, or little painted balloons, buoyed up for the nonce with a puff of inflammable gas; they rather seem, as it has been expressed by one of his most authoritative critics, "to escape as unconsciously from the essence of the earth and air as the scent from a violet or the music from a bird."[1] When he writes, he is not doing a thing to make you stare, or to make himself feel as if he were out of the body for a season; he is merely living out his life—he is merely achieving

[1] Hutton, p. 56.

the *bildung* or the culture which Nature meant for his life-task, when she drew out his members marvellously in the womb. And what is this "culture," which certain persons in this country have hastily construed into a monstrous intellectual idolatry and sinful self-worship?[1] as if a nature so

---

[1] Among those who have taken up this notion—a notion, in my opinion, as superficial as it is uncharitable—I am sorry to name Mr Hutton, in various passages of his otherwise admirable Essay. My view of the matter is, no doubt, directly antagonistic to the general current of British opinion on the subject; but shallow, superficial opinions, especially when aided by natural prejudices, are as common on all complex subjects as the atmosphere of Glasgow or Sheffield is full of smoke; and among English critics who think with me that the more charitable view of the character of the great poet on this point is the true one, I am happy to be able to name Carlyle's well-known friend, John Stirling. The following extract is taken from 'The Journal of Caroline Fox,' ch. viii. p. 169: "With regard to Goethe's character, the more Stirling examines, the less he believes in his having wilfully trifled with the feelings of women: with regard to his selfishness, he holds that he did but give the fullest, freest scope for the exercise of his gift; and as we are the gainers thereby, we cannot call it selfishness. When on an expedition with Carlyle to Hampton Court, the great Scotsman was in one of his gloomy humours and finding fault with everything, which made Stirling act on the defensive with equal universality. At last Carlyle shook his head and pronounced, '*Woe to them that are at ease in Zion.*' At which uncharitable outburst, Stirling was reminded of a poem which Goethe has translated, which introduces the character of a dead dog, which one after another approaches, expressing disgust at the smell, the appearance, &c., of the

keenly sympathetic and so widely social as Goethe's could have dreamt of a human culture as a thing possible, made up merely of intellectual dexterities and artistic presentations, without the fine bond of love, the sweetness of social intercourse, and the expansive joy of a large dispensing faculty. By *bildung* or culture Goethe meant nothing less than that high human-godlike ideal set up for us in the text of the great Teacher when he says, "BE YE THEREFORE PERFECT, EVEN AS YOUR FATHER WHO IS IN HEAVEN IS PERFECT;" which, as absolute perfection to mortal men is impossible, practically means that it is every man's duty to make the most of himself that he can with the faculties he possesses and the circumstances in which he is placed; and whosoever does this, may retire from the scene with the consoling consciousness that he has led a perfect human life, in a spiritual sense, and it may be also a prosperous life, as the world is accustomed to estimate prosperity. Goethe did both; and with the exception of the human failings here and there, which I have not been anxious to cloak, he may well deserve to be studied by our generation, and to be handed down to long generations as the model of a perfectly wise and virtuous man.

poor animal. At last Christ passes, looks on it, and says, ' What beautiful white teeth it has !' "

LIFE, CHARACTER, AND MORALS

Grau, theurer freund, ist alle Theorie;
Doch grün des Lebens goldner Baum.

THE WISDOM OF GOETHE.

LIFE, CHARACTER, AND MORALS.

The Problem of Life.

MAN's highest virtue always is as much as possible to rule external circumstances, and as little as possible to let himself be ruled by them. Life lies before us, as a huge quarry before the architect: he deserves not the name of architect except, out of this fortuitous mass, he can combine, with the greatest economy, suitableness, and durability, some form, the pattern of which originated in his own soul. All things without us,—nay, I may add, all things within us,—are mere elements; but deep in the inmost shrine of our nature lies the creative force, which out of these can produce what they were meant to be, and which leaves us neither sleep nor rest, till in one way or another, without us or within us, this product has taken shape.

Doubt.

Doubt of any kind can be removed by nothing but action.

Action.

To be active is the primary vocation of man. All the intervals in which he is obliged to rest, he should employ in gaining clearer knowledge of external things, for this will in its turn facilitate action.

Deliberation.

Long considerations are commonly a proof that we have not the point to be determined clearly in our eye; precipitate proceedings, that we do not know it.

Clearness and Decision.

I reverence the individual who understands distinctly what he wishes; who unweariedly advances, who knows the means conducive to his object, and can seize and use them. How far his object may be great or little, may merit praise or censure, is a secondary consideration with me. A great part of all the misery and mischief that we find in the world arises from the fact that men are too remiss to get a proper knowledge of their object in life, and, when they do know it, to work intensely in attaining it. They seem to me like people who have taken up a notion, that they must and will erect a tower, and who yet expend on the foundation no more material and labour than would be sufficient for a hut.

Retrospection.

Everything that happens to us leaves some trace behind; everything contributes imperceptibly to make us what we are. Yet it is often dangerous to take a strict account of it. For either we grow proud and negligent, or downcast and dispirited; and both are equally injurious in their consequences. The surest plan is just to do the nearest task that lies before us.

Earnestness.

Without earnestness there is nothing to be done in life; yet even among the people whom we call men of culture, but little earnestness is often to be found: in labours and employments, in arts, nay, even in recreations, they plant themselves, if I may say so, in an attitude of self-defence; they live, as they read a heap of newspapers, only to be done with them; they remind one of that young Englishman at Rome, who told, with a contented air, one evening in some company, that "to-day he had despatched six churches and two galleries." They wish to know and learn a multitude of things, and not seldom exactly those things with which they have the least concern; and they never see that hunger is not appeased by snapping at the air. When I become acquainted with a man my first inquiry is: With what does he occupy himself, and how, and with what degree of perseverance? The answer regulates the interest which I take in that man for life.

Madness.

Nothing more exposes us to MADNESS than distinguishing ourselves from others, and nothing more contributes to maintain our common-sense than living in the common way with multitudes of men.

For man there is but one great misfortune, when some idea lays hold of him, which exerts no influence upon active life, or still more, which withdraws him from it.

The Popular Estimate.

The world has a particular way of acting towards public persons of acknowledged merit; it gradually begins to be indifferent to them, and to favour talents which are new, though far inferior; it makes excessive requisitions on the former, and accepts of anything with approbation from the latter.

Self-knowledge.

How can a man learn to know himself? By reflection never, only by action. In the measure in which thou seekest to do thy duty shalt thou know what is in thee. But what is thy duty? the demand of the hour.

What to Hope for in Life.

Capable, active man, be worthy of thyself and expect:

From the great, .	Grace.
From the powerful, . . .	Favour.
From the active and the good, .	Help.
From the many, . . .	Liking.
From individuals,	Love.

Aim of Life.

Every man must think for himself, and he will always find upon his path some truth, or at least a kind of truth, that will help him through life; yet he dare not allow himself to drift; he must be self-controlled—mere naked instinct does not befit a man.

Circumstances and Character.

A man is not little when he finds it difficult to cope with circumstances, but when circumstances overmaster him.

Moderation.

Unlimited activity, of whatever kind, must end in bankruptcy.

Abstract ideas and great conceit are ever on the road to produce terrible catastrophes.

The Present.

It is difficult to do justice to the present. Commonplace characters in the present cause us *ennui;* the good give us not a little to bear; and the bad we must often drag along with us, whether we will or not.

The Mission of Life.

Every extraordinary man has a certain mission which he is called upon to accomplish. If he has fulfilled it, he is no longer needed upon earth in the same form, and Providence uses him for some other purpose. Thus it was with Napoleon and many others. Mozart died in his six-and-thirtieth year; Raphael at the same age; Byron only a little older. But all these had perfectly fulfilled their mission, and it was time for them to depart, that other people might still have something to do in a world made to last a long while.

Riches.

Every one that can administer what he possesses has enough; and to be wealthy is a burdensome affair, unless you have it wisely under your fingers.

The Well-bred Man.

A well-bred carriage is difficult to imitate; for in strictness it is negative, and it implies a long-continued previous training. You are not required to exhibit in your manner anything that betokens dignity; for by this means you are like to run into formality and haughtiness: you are rather to avoid whatever is undignified and vulgar. You are never to forget yourself; are to keep a constant watch upon yourself and others; to forgive nothing that is faulty in your own conduct, in that of others neither to forgive too little nor too much. Nothing must appear to touch you, nothing to agitate: you must never overhurry yourself, must ever keep yourself composed, retaining still an outward calmness, whatever storms may rage within. The noble character at certain moments may resign himself to his emotions; the well-bred man never. The latter is like a man dressed in fair and spotless clothes: he will not lean on anything; every person will beware of rubbing on him. He distinguishes himself from others, yet he may not stand apart. The well-bred man of rank, in spite of every separation, always seems united with the people round him; he is never to be stiff or uncomplying; he is always to appear the first, and never to insist on so appearing.

It is clear then that to seem well-bred, a man must actually be so. It is also clear why women are generally more expert at taking up the air of breeding than the other sex; why courtiers and soldiers catch it more easily than other men.

Social Intercourse. Faults and Follies.

The passion for looking into the FUTURE is so common because we have a pleasure in turning the accidental element of which it is full, by help of quiet wishes and guesses, into something that tells in our favour.

People may live as much retired from the world as they please, but sooner or later before they are aware they will find themselves debtor or creditor to somebody.

To communicate our feelings and sentiments is natural; to take up what is communicated just as it is communicated is CULTURE.

No man would talk much in society, if he were fully conscious how often he misunderstands other people.

When we repeat what we have heard in CONVERSATION, we do it with some change which generally proceeds from some misunderstanding.

He who takes a prominent part in conversation in

company without to a certain extent flattering the hearers, excites ill-will or displeasure.

Every word uttered in conversation naturally brings out its contrary.

Contradiction and gross flattery equally destroy good conversation. That society is the most pleasant in which the persons composing it habitually display a cheerful respect for one another.

There is nothing by which men display their character so much as in what they consider RIDICULOUS.

To the man of superficial cleverness almost everything readily takes a ridiculous aspect; to the man of thought almost nothing is really ridiculous.

An old gentleman was blamed for continuing to pay attention to young ladies. "It is the only means I have," he replied, "to keep myself young, and every one is ready to do that."

People will allow their faults to be spread out before them, nay, will suffer various castigations on their account; but when they are called upon to give them up, then they become impatient.

Certain faults are necessary for the existence of the

individual. It would, for instance, be disagreeable for us if our old friends gave up certain peculiarities which may be gross faults.

People say he will die soon, when they see a man doing something contrary to his usual habits.

What sort of faults may we retain, nay, even cherish in ourselves? Those faults which are rather pleasant than offensive to others.

PASSIONS are defects or virtues in the highest power.

Our passions are at once elevated and softened by confession. In nothing perhaps is the golden mean so desirable as in the practice of confidence and reticence towards those whom we love.

Life.

He is already dead who lives only to keep himself alive.

Present and Future.

Do I live for no other purpose than to think about living? Am I to deny myself the enjoyment of the present moment, in order to make myself certain of the following moment, and when it comes, to be cheated out of its fair promise with all sorts of whims and worries?

Society and Conversation.

In SOCIETY every man is taken for what he gives himself out to be; but he must give himself out for something. Better to be slightly disagreeable than altogether insignificant.

We can never learn what sort of persons people are, when they come to us; we must go to them, if we would know what stuff they are made of, and how they manage or mismanage their surroundings.

I find it quite natural that when people present themselves to us in the position of VISITORS, we should have many things to object to them, that, as soon as they leave us, we should come out with some not very charitable remarks; for we have in those circumstances a sort of right to measure them by the value we put upon ourselves. Even sensible and moderate persons find difficulty on such occasions in abstaining from unkindly comments. If, on the other hand, we live for some days with other people, and observe how they comport themselves in a well-ordered establishment, only stupidity or malice could delight to find faults, where so much worthy of admiration is presented.

The company of chaste WOMEN is the proper atmosphere of good manners.

A MILITARY MAN, when he is a person of intelligence and knowledge, has advantages, both in life and society, superior to what most other men enjoy. Even a rough and uncultured soldier may present himself as he is, without giving the same offence that an equal amount of roughness in a person of a less favoured profession would cause; and besides, in the character of soldiers, there is generally, behind the outward display of rude strength, a substratum of good-humour, which gives a pleasant seasoning to their *gaucheries*. On the other hand, a rude civilian is of all men the most disagreeable; for the function which he has to perform in society is of a nature that naturally should cultivate a certain delicate tact, the farthest removed from anything like coarseness.

No man with SPECTACLES on nose would enter into a familiar conversation with a lady, if he knew that women lose all inclination to speak confidentially with a man, when they have to encounter a pair of glass lenses instead of a living eye.

There is no external expression of POLITENESS which has not a root in the moral nature of man. Forms of politeness, therefore, should never be inculcated on young persons without letting them understand the moral ground on which all such forms rest.

A man's MANNERS are a mirror in which he shows his likeness to the intelligent observer.

There is a POLITENESS of the heart; this is closely allied to LOVE. Those who possess this purest fountain of natural politeness find it easy to express the same in forms of outward propriety.

To preserve our place and our peace of mind with pleasure in the face of the decided superiority of another, our competitor in the same sphere of action, there is only one charm, and that is LOVE.

No man, they say, is a HERO to his *valet de chambre*. But the reason of this is that a hero can be recognised only by a hero. And in this way, no doubt, the valet will have no difficulty in estimating the high and low as they are manifested in the person of other valets.

There is no greater consolation for a certain class of commonplace people than that men of overtopping genius are not immortal.

Men even of the greatest genius acknowledge the

influence of the age to which they belong by a certain characteristic weakness.

Men, for the most part, are looked upon as more dangerous than they are.

FOOLS and sensible men are equally innocuous. It is in the half fools and the half wise that the great danger lies.

Critical Moments.

At certain epochs of our life we find ourselves in circumstances, that, while they press upon us, and even seem altogether to weigh us down, at the same time give us the opportunity, nay, impose on us the DUTY, to elevate ourselves, and by so doing fulfil the purpose of the Divine Being in our creation; for in behaving manfully under such circumstances, we are forced on the one hand to assert to the full all the effective force that is in us, and on the other hand to deny ourselves persistently, in so far as this may be necessary for the maintenance of our position.

Self-control.

From time to time I meet a young man in whom I can see nothing to object to; only I feel anxious when I observe such a finely equipped fellow ready to swim with the stream; and here I am always forced to make the remark that the rudder is given into the hand of man in his frail skiff, not that he may be at the mercy of the waves, but that he may follow the dictates of a will directed by intelligence.

Love.

Hatred and ill-will confine the spectator to the mere surface of what he sees, let him be ever so acute; but when great perspicacity is associated with kindliness and love, the observer may pierce beyond the mere shell of men and of the world, and under happy influences may hope to solve the highest problems.

Means and End.

Men get out of their reckoning, both in respect of themselves and others, by treating the mere *means* as an *end;* and under this delusion out of sheer activity springs mere barrenness, or it may be something altogether monstrous.

Truth.

Men sometimes seem vexed that, after all, TRUTH is so very simple an affair; they ought to bear in mind that, simple as it is, they have generally trouble enough before they can apply it to any practical purpose.

Old Age.

We must not take the faults of our youth into our old age; for old age brings with it its own defects.

Character.

We have much need of a man like Lessing; for how did this man support himself so high in the reputation of his countrymen? By his character and his consistency alone. There are many men as long-headed and as cultivated as he; but where will you find such a character?

Reverence.

Many men have plenty of cleverness, and plenty of knowledge, but they are at the same time full of vanity; and, in order to obtain from the shallow multitude the reputation of a *bel esprit*, they fling aside all shame and all reverence, and nothing is holy before their reckless wit.

Madame de Genlis was therefore quite right to protest against the unbridled licentiousness of Voltaire. For at bottom, however clever his profane witticisms may be, they do no good to the world,—they form a foundation for nothing; nay, they may even do much harm by confusing those who are weak in the faith, and taking from under them their only stay.

And then, what truly do we know,—and how little can we attain to with all our wit?

Now.

"I feel myself," said ECKERMANN, "gradually leaving my ideal and theoretic tendencies, and more and more able to appreciate the value of the present moment."

"Only persist in this," said GOETHE, "and HOLD FAST BY THE PRESENT. Every situation—nay, every moment—is of infinite value, for it is the representative of a whole eternity."

Knowledge of Men.

What would be the use of culture, if we did not try to control our natural tendencies? It is a great folly to hope that other men will harmonise with us; I have never hoped this. I have always regarded each man as an independent individual, whom I endeavoured to study, and to understand with all his peculiarities, but from whom I had a right to demand no further sympathy. In this way I have been enabled to converse with every man; and thus alone is produced the knowledge of various characters, and the dexterity necessary for the conduct of life. For it is in a conflict with natures opposed to his own that a man must collect his strength to fight his way through life; and thus all our different sides are brought out and developed, so that we soon feel ourselves a match for every foe.

Self-importance.

We cannot too soon convince ourselves how very easily we may be dispensed with in the world. What important personages we conceive ourselves to be! We think that it is we alone who animate the circle in which we move; that in our absence, life, nourishment, and breath will make a general pause; and, alas! the void which occurs is scarce remarked, so quickly is it filled up again; and it is well for even our dearest friends when they soon recover their composure; when they say each to himself, there where thou art, there where thou remainest, accomplish what thou canst; be busy, be courteous, and let the present scene delight thee.

Children.

In speaking of a child, we have pleasure not only from what we see, but even more from what we hope for.

Happiness.

Who is the happiest person?—he whose nature asks for nothing that the world does not wish and use.

Misfortune.

Misfortune, when we look upon it with our eye, is

smaller than when our imagination entertains the evil, and gives it a lodgment in the inner chamber of the soul.

Judgment of Persons.

We never should inspect the conduct of men, unless we at the same time take an interest in improving it; and it is through action only that we can ever be in a condition to inspect and watch ourselves.

Character.

The formation of his character is not, as it ought to be, the chief concern with every man. Many wish merely to find a sort of recipe for comfort, directions for acquiring riches, or whatever good they aim at.

Slow Growth.

He in whom there is much to develop will be later in acquiring true perceptions of himself and of the world. There are few who possess at once thought and the capacity of action. Thought expands but slackens; action animates but confines.

Talent.

We should guard against a talent which we cannot hope to practise in perfection. Improve it as we may, we shall always in the end, when the merit of the great masters has become apparent to us, painfully lament the loss of time and strength devoted to it.

Our Principles.

What we call our principles are often just a supplement to our peculiar manner of existence. We delight to clothe our errors in the garb of universal laws; to attribute them to irresistibly appointed causes.

Guidance.

It is inconceivable how much a man of true culture can accomplish for himself and others, if, without attempting to rule, he is in a position to be the guardian over many; can induce them to do that in season, which they are at any rate disposed enough to do; can guide them to their objects, which in general they see with due distinctness, though they miss the road to them. Let us make a league for this; it is no empty enthusiasm, but an idea which may be fully carried out—is often carried out indeed, only with imperfect consciousness, by people of benevolence and worth.

Popularity.

The world sees only the reflection of merit. Therefore when you come to know a really great man intimately, you may as often find him above, as below, his reputation.

Self-estimate.

It is right that a man, when he first enters on life, should think highly of himself, should determine to attain many eminent distinctions, and endeavour to make all things possible; but, when his education has advanced to a certain point, it is advantageous for him that he learn to lose himself among a mass of men—that he learn, for the sake of others, to forget himself in an activity prescribed by duty. It is then that he first becomes acquainted with himself; for it is conduct alone that compares us with others.

The Work of Life.

Art is long, life short, judgment difficult, opportunity fleeting. To act is easy; to think is hard; to act according to our thinking is troublesome. Every beginning is cheerful; the threshold is the place of expectation. The boy stands astonished; his impressions guide him; he learns sportfully; seriousness comes on him by surprise.

Words and Deeds.

Words are good; but they are not the best. The best is not to be explained by words. The spirit in which we act is the great matter. Action can be understood, and again represented by the spirit alone. No man knows what he is doing, while he acts rightly; but of what is wrong we are always conscious.

Judge not.

How can men judge rightly of our actions, appearing as they do but singly, or in fragments to them? actions of which they see the smallest part; while good and bad take place in secret, and, for the most part, nothing comes to light but an indifferent show.

Self-knowledge.

There are persons quite unstable and incapable of all improvement, who frequently accuse themselves in the bitterest manner, confessing and deploring their faults with extreme ingenuousness, though they possess not the smallest power within them to retire from the course along which the irresistible tendency of their nature is dragging them.

Explanations.

I hate all explanations; they who make them deceive either themselves or the other party—generally both.

Co-operation.

Honest, clear, and unselfish co-operation for the realisation of the good and true, that lies between two extremes, is seldom to be met with. What we do meet with is obstinate adherence to an obsolete and soulless tradition on the one hand, and a rash lust for change on the other; retardation without reason, and haste without safety.

Self-praise.

"Self-praise hath a bad smell." Very true; but what sort of a smell dispraise and misrepresentation of others may have, on this point the public nose says nothing.

Love.

It is said that like loves like; but it is said also that love goes by contraries. Both sayings are true. There is a class of men who are attracted only by those who are like themselves; and another class who are powerfully drawn towards that which is most opposite to themselves.

Self-contradiction.

An antagonism within ourselves—a sort of self-contradiction,—is often not to be avoided. We must face it, and endeavour to adjust the opposing claims how best we may. On the other hand, contradiction from other parties, had, on the general case, better be let alone. Their negative attitude is their business, not ours.

Ignorance.

Nothing is more terrible than ignorance with spurs on.

Corruption of Human Nature.

Every man bears something within him that, if it were publicly pronounced, would excite a feeling of aversion.

Man.

Man would not be the aristocratic creature that he is in the world, were he not too aristocratic for it.

Judgment.

A man whose clear intellect can form a perfectly correct decision about the matter before him, may err greatly by enunciating such particular decision with a kind of universal application; whereas, in truth, the judgments of the understanding are properly of force but once, and that in the special case, and become inaccurate in some degree when applied to any other case.

Old Age.

Old age must rest content with being deprived of one of the greatest of all human rights, the right of being judged by our equals.

Self-limitation.

The smallest man may be complete, if he confine his activity within the natural range of his capacities and dexterities; but even superior talents will be obscured, defeated, and destroyed, if this indispensable instinct of self-limitation is wanting. Mistakes arising from this defect will come more and more to the front in modern times; for who shall be able to satisfy the demands of an age, living under the stimulus of a constant high pressure, and the excitement of a hot-spurred progression?

Conscience and Action.

The man of action has no conscience in the moment of action; only the observer passes a severe judgment.

Morality of the World.

The moral sentiment of what is called the world, is made up in great measure of ill-will and envy.

Rule of Life.

Wouldst thou be a happy liver,
Let the past be past for ever!
Fret not, when prigs and pedants bore you;
Enjoy the good that's set before you;
But chiefly hate no man; the rest
Leave thou to God, who knows what's best.

Life the School of Manhood.

A noble man may to a narrow sphere
Not owe his training. In his country he
And in the world must learn to be at home,

And bear both praise and blame, and by long proof
Of contest and collision nicely know
Himself and others,—not in solitude,
Cradling his soul in dreams of fair conceit.
A foe will not, a true friend dare not, spare him;
And thus in strife of well-tried powers he grows,
Feels what he is, and feels himself a man.

The World, and how to Use it.

Live with the world whoso has nerve
To make the world his purpose serve;
But, if you leave your lofty level
To do the world's vile command,
You were as well to let the devil
Keep all your gear in hand.

The Wisdom of Life.

Use well the moment; what the hour
Brings for thy use is in thy power;
And what thou best canst understand,
Is just the thing lies nearest to thy hand.

Home.

He is the happiest man, be he the king,
Or be the meanest subject, whoso knows
The comfort of a home administered
By wisely practised hands.

Pride and Insolence.

The race of men is far too weak to stand
Upon a proud uncustomed height, and feel
No giddiness.

Variety and Perfection.

Like be none to another, but like be each to the highest :
How to do that?—let each in his own sphere be complete.

Little and Big.

Art thou little, do that little well, and for thy comfort know,
The biggest man can do his biggest work no better than just so.

Self-knowledge.

Know myself?—what profit could that bring?
   I'd shudder at myself and flap my wing,
And fly ten leagues away from such a hateful thing.

What the World wants with you.

  Don't quarrel with mankind,
    That they are blind
  To scrolls of merit blazoned on your banners.

They want nor thought nor sentiment,
    Well content
With pleasant words and polished manners.

Secrecy.

Your purpose told to others is your own
No longer; with your will once set at large
Blind accident will sport. Who would command
Mankind, must hold them fast by swift surprise;
Nay more,—even with the strongest will he fails
To do great things, crossed by a thousand wills
With petty contradiction.

Love—Liking and Disliking.

What mystery doth the magnet move?
As great, no greater than my hate or love.

Find one quite like yourself, and you
Will run, abhorrent, from the view.

Lads dance with lasses—why? 'tis just because
Not like to like, but like to unlike draws.

The Whole or a Part?

To live a whole in thine own self is life's most lofty
    style,
But if thy wing mounts not so high, thou art not
    therefore vile;

Go join thee to some noble whole, and be a part of
    him,
Content, who cannot be the head, to be a useful limb.

Hatred and Envy.

Envy's the foil to fair prosperity;
And hatred teaches us, when foes abound,
To keep our armour on.

Self-dependence.

Thy tented welkin, Jove, enshroud
With vapoury cloud,
And, like a boy, with lusty strokes,
Who crops the thistle's crown,
O'er mountain-peaks and aged oaks,
Come blustering down;
Yet must thou yield
To me my earth,
My hut which mine own hands did build,
And mine own hearth,
Whose blazing glee
Thou enviest me.

Nothing more vile the sun below,
Than your host of gods I know!
Ye nourish in most sorry guise,
With tribute base of sacrifice,

And breath of prayer,
Your majesty;
And would starve sheer,
Were there not here,
Children and beggars, a servile crew,
Hopeful fools to flatter you.

When I was a little boy,
And laughed and wept, I knew not why,
Up to the sun and to the sky,
Wistful I cast my wandering eye,
As if above there were an ear,
My plaint to hear;
A heart like mine in yonder pole,
To bind the wounds o' the anguished soul.

Received I then aught aid from you,
Against the haughty Titan crew?
Who then from death did set me free,
And slavery?
Thyself achieved it with thy inborn art,
Thou holy, glowing heart!
But, young and artless, thou didst pour
Thy gushing thanks (fond fool!) before
The sleeper there above.

I reverence thee! for what?
Hast thou ever in mercy known
To soothe the laden spirit's groan?

Thou ever stilled the tears that start,
When doubts perplex the heart?
Hath not, to the full-grown man,
Forged me Time's all-mighty plan,
And eternal Destiny,
Lord both of thee and me.

Deem'dst thou, belike, that I should hate my life,
And into deserts flee,
Because I could not see,
All blossoms of my dreamings rife?
Here sit I, and with life inspire
A race that shall be like their sire;
Who shall know beneath the skies,
To suffer, and to weep,
To enjoy, and to rejoice,
And thee and thine even so despise,
As I do!

Curiosity.

Far from me be the lust to blame with rash condemnation,
Harmless instincts implanted by Nature, the bountiful
   mother;
For what Reason would grope for in vain, spontaneous
   impulse
Ofttimes achieves at a stroke with light and pleasure-
   ful guidance.

Tell me this—if the eye with curious greed did not wander
Hither and thither to see, how then we could reach in our knowledge
All the wonders outspread in the beautiful world before us?
First we seek for the new with eager delight, and the useful
Then with assiduous toil,—and then the good, which alone can
Raise to his level the man, and add to his worth in the raising.
Nature gave to the young a careless light disposition,
Witless of danger, and wise to brush the witness of sorrow
Swift from the eye, till it passes away like showers in the spring-time.
Him not less we admire the full-grown man, whom it likes not
Careless to live for the hour, but who firmly, with sober conviction,
Works through rough and through smooth with proud persistent exertion;
He produces the good, and he compensates the evil.

Consistency and Firmness.

He who in slippery times unstable lives and unsteady,
Maketh the bad to be worse, and spreads the contagion around him;

But with firmness of will who stands, and holds to
    his purpose,
Maketh the world his clay, and shapes all men to his
    service.

Death.

The piteous image of Death stands
Not to the wise as a terror, and not as the end to the
    pious.
Wisely the wise man is driven from thought of death
    into action;
Wisely the pious from death draws hope of bliss for
    the future.
Each is wise in his way; and death to life is trans-
    muted
Wisely by both.

Work.

Shoot your own thread right through the earthly
    tissue,
Bravely: and leave the gods to find the issue.

Receptiveness and Projectiveness.

Wouldst thou live well in the land,
Take two wallets in thy hand,
This to gather what you find,
That to give with willing mind;

Just as princes when they travel,
With heavy hand lay on the charges,
And then from overflowing founts
Of Royal bounty make a largess!

Love of Fame.

For living men to live for fame,
Is to nurse fret, and hunt for blame;
And for your posthumous reputation,
When you have joined the ghostly nation,
Trust me, when Fame beneath the sod,
Has slept one hundred years, 'tis odd,
If one man in a million knows
How you disturbed the world's repose.

Pride and Ignorance.

Who rides so fast? Dame Ignorance
And Lady Pride. Well, never mind them;
They'll find some day, as they advance,
Shame and Reproach close tacked behind them!

Rule of Life.

Like the star
That shines afar,
Without haste
And without rest,
Let each man wheel with steady sway,
Round the task that rules the day,
And do his best!

If.

"This young man I might like," quoth the dainty maiden: "that other,
Noble and good though he be, hits not my fancy at all:
But this third I would take to my heart, if I only could get him;
If, O sorrowful *if!* all the best things have an *If.*"

Repentance.

If it be noble in our hearts to keep
The memory of our faults, and weigh them well,
And in their room plant virtues, nevermore
Can it be right and praiseful, with long fret
For past misdeeds to undermine the heart,
And lame the springs of action!

Self-love.

Other men's children we love not quite so well as our own, and
Error that's born of our blood closely we hug to our heart.

Life.

Counsel and guidance you ask; try this, and try that and the other:
Living will teach you to live better than preacher or book.

Saints and Sinners.

Greatest saints we know have been the most kindly to sinners:
Here I'm a saint with the best; sinners I never could hate.

Evil cures Evil.

Tell me how to get rid of the sparrows, grumbled the gardener;
Sparrows, and beetles to boot, beetles and grubs in the ground;
Moles and wasps and worms, the slimy spawn of the Devil;
Let them alone, and they will eat one another, be sure!

The best Vantage-ground.

Life's vantage-ground, the best I know,
Is this—to own the merits of your foe.

A Hypochondrist.

The Devil take the people! plague
On all the human race!
And thus I vow to shut the door
On all the vermin, nevermore
To look them in the face!

But scarcely had I flung my ban
On all the hateful human clan,
And let them go, to find their level
With God, themselves, or with the Devil,
When I met this one, and that other,
And said,—God bless you, my good brother!

Impatience.

Why seek at once to dive into
The depth of all that meets your view?
Wait for the melting of the snow,
And then you'll see what lies below.

Society.

A quiet learned man from dinner
Came back one day, a weary sinner:
"How did you like the guests?"—"The guests,"
He said, "were men, and the host well fed them,
But had they been books, I wouldn't have read them!"

Mundus vult decipi, decipiatur.

Let doctors dispute, and logicians conclude,
And pedants protest with a frown on their brow;
From the birth of old Time all the wise and the good
Agree in the gospel I preach to you now,—
If you wait till the fool shall grow wise, you will wait
Till the round shall grow square, and the crooked grow straight;
Treat the fool like a fool, and you'll give him his due.

Merlin the wizard, when I was a youth,
From his radiant sepulchre, told me the truth
With oracular voice, as I tell it to you,—
If you wait till the fool shall grow wise, you will wait
Till the round shall grow square, and the crooked
    grow straight;
Treat the fool as a fool, and you give him his due.

From the shrines of the rock in far Indian land,
From the tombs of the kings 'neath the Memphian
    sand,
On the wings of the wind this old oracle flew,—
If you wait till the fool shall grow wise, you will wait
Till the round shall grow square, and the crooked
    grow straight;
Treat the fool like a fool—'tis his right, and his due.

Judgment.

I can promise to be sincere; to be impartial, not.

Prosperity.

Men may bear much from fits of harsh severity,
But not a long run of unmixed prosperity.

Good-humour.

Give me the man who bears a big load lightly,
And looks on grave things with a blithe face brightly;

And when he flings a stinging jest on others,
Laughs at himself, and says,—*We all are brothers!*

Love.

Whatever stores of fact or fable
   You've gathered to inform your soul,
Will be mere discord worse than Babel,
   Unless pure love unite the whole!

Old Age.

An old man is a kind of King Lear.
The men with thee that bravely strove
Are wandered far, or gone above;
And they who leant upon thy breast,
On other cushions now find rest.
Young folks for the young folks are here,
And have no word to say to thee;
Nor thou hast right to say to them,
Come boys, be old and wise with me!

Secrecy.

If a strong arm and a brave, fearless spirit
Are qualities that most become a man,
Deep secrecy, and firm rein on the tongue,
Suit him no less; divine of goddesses,
Ruler of peoples, counsellor of princes,
Wise Reticence, that through the storms of life
Helmed my frail bark securely.

Wilfulness.

The man who brooks no self-control fulfils
Not the first simplest duty of all men
To make wise choice of food and drink, which he,
As being free from brutish bonds, should do
Freely and wisely; but we see him rather
Even as a child, the slave to every taste
That lords his palate. He disdains to mix
His wine with water, and with hasty gulp
Swills all strong drinks and high-spiced liquors down
His inconsiderate throat, and after talks
Of bad digestion, fevered blood, and dull
Despondency, and passion's fitful sway;
And then he rates dame Nature, and harsh Fate,
Not his own folly. Let him chance be sick,
He calls a doctor. "Well. Sir Doctor, I
You see lie sickly here, God knows for why;
But you must know the cure, and you must work
My swift recovery." "Well," replies the leech,
"This food avoid and that." "Nay, but I can't."
"Then take this draught." "No; that tastes as dis-
 tilled
From Stygian pools: against such drug my whole
Nature rebels." "Well, if you will not own
The grateful force of drugs, one cure remains:
Drink water." "Water!—no, not I!—no dog
Could bite me into hydrophobia
More than the hate of water I was born with."

"Well, then, I cannot help you." "Cannot?—why?"
"From day to day your illness must grow worse,
And, though it kill you not, will heap you up
With highest power of pains." "O most wise leech!
You are a doctor; my disease you know,
And you should know the cure, and how to come
So softly with the cunning of your craft;
But you but shame the art which you profess
By drugs that work more pain than the disease."
Who could believe such brainless talk from men,
And yet we hear it!

The Temporary and the Eternal.

Nothing may perish
  Beneath the sky;
All things have their issues
  That mortals try.
We are here for a day,
To stamp on the clay,
A part of ourselves
  That never may die.

Delay in Business.

Why this delay?—only who runs may win!
Well, laziness, you know, is not my sin;
But, somehow, when great things I would achieve,
I find a fool from whom I must ask leave.

Danger.

Success
Snatched boldly from the moment, not the note
Of fearful apprehension wields the reins
That sway the course of danger.

Occupation.

If I am banned from thinking, and from doing,
Life is no life to me. Forbid the fine
Silk-weaving worm to weave its web, for that
He spins himself to death, and may not cease
Till from his life of life he hath spun out
A costly thread to coffin him all round!
Oh that a god might grant to us some day,
Even like this worm, to spin ourselves to death,
And in a larger, sunnier world reborn,
To flap our wings with joy!

Miracle.

When in the world a miracle appears,
'Tis faithful loving hearts that work the wonder.

Love and Friendship.

True FRIENDSHIP shows its worth in stern refusal
At the right moment; and strong LOVE sometimes
Heaps the loved one with ruin, when it serves
The will more than the weal of who demands.

And thou, my friend, as now I know thee, seemest
To hold that good for which thou hotly wishest,
And to transmute into a fact the fancy
That was the moment's birth. 'Twas often seen
That he who errs doth strive to compensate
By violence his lack of strength and will;
I am thy friend, and hold it for my duty
To slow the speed that spurs thee to thy wrong.

Rejuvenescence.

Not in the grave, or in the world beyond,
A noble man looks for new springs of life,
But looks within, and with strange wonder finds
A new life there that makes him young again.

Love.

If heaven were mine, with only me in heaven,
Few hells could be more hard for me to live in!

Knowledge of Men.

No man fears men, but he who knows them not;
And he who shuns them may not hope to know them.

Patience.

Nay, don't lose heart; small men and mighty nations
Have learned a great deal when they practise patience.

Lies.

Would you tell lies to cheat the people? No!
I'm a plain man, and tell you plainly—No!
But if you will tell lies, cut a broad slice
With a free hand, and don't be over-nice!

The Golden Age.

My friend, your golden age is gone,
But good men still can bring it back again;
Rather, if I must speak the truth, I'll say
The golden age of which the poet sings
In flattering phrase, this age at no time was
On Earth one whit more than it is to-day;
And, if it ever was, 'twas only so,
As all good men can bring it back to-morrow.

Self-knowledge.

'Tis no doubt pleasant
Ourselves with our own selves to occupy,
Were but the profit equal to the pleasure.
Inwardly no man can his inmost self
Discern; the gauge that from himself he takes
Measures him now too small, and now too great.
Only in man man knows himself, and only
Life teaches each man what each man is worth.

Quarrels.

When two men quarrel, who owns the coolest head
Is most to blame.

Good Society.

READER.

What means this rabble of low people here—
Quack doctor, juggler, beggar, gondolier?
Hast seen no good society, that you
Should waste good verse on such uncultured crew?

POET.

Oh yes! your good society, in the mint
　Of courts 'tis coined, and very well I know it;
So fine and featureless, it leaves no hint
　For smallest touch of nature to a poet.

Prophets.

Who spouts his message to the wilderness
Lightens his soul, and feels one burden less:
But to the people preach, and you will find
They'll pay you back with thanks ill to your mind.

Monuments.

The marble bears his name, and tells his story.
But you'll forgive me, if I hint the truth:
You gild the monument in honest sooth,
Not for his honour, but for your own glory.

Envy.

Envy must be : e'en let her feed her grudge!
Truth will shine out, when time shall be the judge;
'Tis an old use that hath been, and will be,
That where the sun his liberal light may throw,
The heat comes with it, and the grass will grow.

Youth.

Who may be proud? the young : for why? the pride
Of life is theirs, and Time is on their side.

Divide et Impera.

Divide and rule, the politician cries ;
Unite and lead, is watchword of the wise.

Slander.

Go north and south on German ground,
    Eastward and westward wander,
Two nasty things you'll find abound—
    Tobacco-smoke, and slander.

Utopia.

Your lazy loon, if dainty pigeons
Up to his mouth well roasted flew,
He would not taste them, no, not he,
Unless well carved and served up too !

Perversity.

An ill-starred devil is the man,
Who will not do the thing he can;
And what he can't, with blind ambition
Will do, and works his own perdition.

To-day.

To-day, to-day, only show valiant face,
And you have gained a hundred days of grace.

Solitude and Society.

In still retreat a thoughtful talent thrives,
But in the stream and current of the world
The character grows strong.

Limits of Humanity.

When the eternal
Father of gods and men
Soweth with kindly hand
Forth from the rolling clouds
Lightnings of blessing
Over the fields of Earth,
Humbly, then, I the last
Hem of his garment kiss,
With the love and the fear
Of a child in my breast.

For with the gods
May no son of man compare :
If upward he soareth,
Touching with head sublime
Stars that eternal shine,
Nowhere he finds there
Place for his foot to stand,
And with him freely
Sport there the birds and clouds.

When he with strong
And marrowy bones stands
On the well-grounded
Base of the solid earth,
Not even then
He dares with the oak compare,
Or with the vine
That clambers around its trunk.

Say what distinguisheth
Gods from the sons of men?
They are as waves
That rolling-on waves flow
In an eternal stream :
Us the wave lifteth,
Us the wave whelmeth,
And we are seen no more.

Small is the ring
That claspeth our life round ;

And generations
On generations
Coming and going,
Add link to link
Of an infinite chain.

The Vocation of Man.

Noble be man,
Friendly and good,
For goodness alone
Stamps him diverse
From all the creatures
That walk the earth.

Hail to the unknown
Mightier beings
Whom we anticipate!
What in the human
Typed we behold
Leads to a faith
In the primal Divine.

For NATURE knows
No feeling for man;
The sun doth shine
On the bad and the good;
On fair and on foul
With indifferent eye
Look moon and stars.

Wind and water,
Thunder and hail,
Rush on their path,
And with hasty clutch
They seize as they pass
This one and that.

Even so FORTUNE
Blindly seizes
Now the light locks
Of innocent boyhood,
Now the bald crown
Of the hoary offender.

Bound by eternal
All-embracing
Iron decrees,
We must accomplish
Each man his fated
Circle of being.

But in the human
Range of his action
MAN, like a god,
May achieve the impossible;
He distinguishes,
Chooses and judges,
And gives to the moment
The stamp of endurance.

He alone
Rewardeth the good,
Chastiseth the bad,
And all extravagant
Random endeavours
Binds with the bond
Of a common design.

And we wisely
Adore the Immortals,
Deeming them brothered
With what is most human,
In the great cosmos,
Willing and working
What in their small lives
Men may achieve.

The noble man
Be friendly and good,
Shaping unwearied
The useful, the right,
Planting before us
A sensible type
Of those beings unseen
Whom by faith we divine!

RELIGION

Wer Gott ahnet ist hoch zu halten;
Denn er wird nie im Schlechten walten.

RELIGION.

Reverence—The Three Stages of Religion.

HEALTHY children, born under favourable influences, bring much into the world with them. Nature has given to every one all he needs for time and eternity; the duty of the educator and trainer is to develop this; and most frequently it develops best when left to itself. But there is one thing no one brings with him into the world, and it is a thing on which everything else depends; that thing by means of which every man that is born into the world becomes truly manly. This thing is REVERENCE; of which there are three kinds, or, if you will, three stages. These we endeavour to implant in the minds of our pupils, with the symbolical accompaniment of three attitudes or postures. The first kind is reverence for that which is above us; and the attitude connected with this is that in which, with the arms crossed over the breast, our pupils are taught to look joyfully towards the heavens. By this we ask from them an acknowledgment that there is a God on high who reflects and reveals Himself in the person of parents, teachers, and superiors. The second type is reverence for that which is beneath us. The hands clasped as though bound, behind the back, the downward, smiling look, in the attitude belonging to this type, indicate that we should look upon the earth graciously and cheerfully; for it is the earth that affords us the means of subsistence, and is the source of innumerable joys, though, along with these, it no doubt brings not seldom disproportionate sufferings. When a man receives any physical hurt, whether by his own fault or innocently; or when another injures him, either of set purpose or accidentally; when in any way harmful terrestrial forces and influences invade him harshly;—let the young person learn to ponder seriously on these things; and let him know that from such dangers he cannot altogether escape so long as he lives. But from this attitude we set our pupil free as soon as possible, the moment we are assured the lesson it is intended to convey has had its proper effect; then we call on him to brace himself like a man, and turning to his comrades, to pit himself against them. Now he stands firm and bold, but not selfishly isolated. Only in conflict with his fellows can the young man learn to face the world. Our third attitude indicates this: standing upright and with forward look, they take their stations no longer singly, but linked together in a row.

From these considerations we see the reason why the tone of mind in the majority of people in the world is so low, and so pregnant with unhappiness: their evil judging and evil talking is but the natural fruit of their want of reverence. Whosoever surrenders himself to this temper learns to despise the world, to hate his neighbour instead of loving him, and even at last to become indifferent to God; and that feeling of proper self-respect and healthy self-assertion, without which a man cannot work effectively in the world, loses itself in conceit and insolence. . . . This reverence, I repeat, we bring not with us into the world; it is the growth of culture. Fear, no doubt, every man brings with him into the world, and naturally enough; not so Reverence. From the earliest times we find in the breast of the lowest savages a fear before the mighty phenomena of Nature, and other inexplicable forces and ominous influences. But this fear is not reverence. We fear an unknown Being or a heaven; this feeling the strong man seeks to overcome, the weak man to escape from; both strive to shake themselves free of it, and think themselves fortunate when they have set it aside for a short time, and their nature has scope to reassert itself as in some measure free and independent. The natural man repeats this operation a million times in his life; he struggles from fear into freedom, and is driven again back into fear; and in the end remains just where he was. To fear is easy but oppressive; to reverence, difficult but full of solace. Only reluctantly does man make up his mind to reverence; or rather he never does so for himself. It is a higher sense, which must be imparted to his nature, and which is self-developed in a few favoured beings, who have on this account been in all ages held as saints, or even as gods. And herein lies the virtue and operative force of all true religions; and of these there are only three, classed according to the object of their worship.

No religion founded upon mere fear comes under any estimation with us. With the reverence which any one allows to sway his soul, he can always retain self-respect, however low he may prostrate himself before a superior; he is not, as in the case of fear, set at variance with himself.

The religion which is founded on reverence for what is above us we call *ethnic*, or, as it is in vulgar English, *heathen*. It is the religion of the nations (ἔθνη), and the first happy deliverance from abject fear. To this class belong all pagan religions, whatever names they may bear. The second type of religion, founded upon the reverence we cherish for what is on a par with ourselves, we call the philosophical; for the philosopher, who takes a central position, must draw down to his level what is above, while he seeks to elevate what is below; and only when in this middle state does he deserve the name of a sage. In so far, then, as he has a clear insight into his relations to his equals, and to all humanity, as also to all his earthly surroundings, whether necessary or casual, does he live, cosmically speaking, in the truth. But now we must speak of the third type, founded on reverence for what is beneath us : this is Christianity ; for in it chiefly is this sentiment dominant. It is the highest step in the ladder of reverence to which humanity can attain ; for, consider only what extraordinary moral force is required to be in a religion, which could not merely let the world drop from its view, claiming for itself a higher home, but could recognise obscurity and poverty, disgrace and contempt, ignominy and misery, suffering and death, as being something godlike ; yea, and could conceive a certain honour even in sin itself, and in crime, transmuting them from hindrances and obstructions into means of positive progress to the saint. Of this sentiment no doubt we find traces in all ages ; but a trace is not the goal ; and once this height has been reached, mankind cannot recur to a lower platform ; and we may thus say that the Christian religion, having once appeared on the earth, cannot disappear ; nor, having once assumed a divine embodiment on the stage of humanity, ever again retreat, and be as if it had not been.

These three types together form the true religion ; and the religious man of highest culture now professes virtually all the three. From these three embodied types springs the consummation of all reverences,—the reverence for one's self; out of which the other three again develop themselves. And so man in this way reaches the highest of which he is capable, and may think of himself as the acme of all that God and nature have produced; may even dwell on this height with a healthy complacency, without being dragged down to the common level by conceit and selfishness. And all this, in fact, however it may appear new to some, exists already in the CREDO of the Christian Churches: for the first article is ethnic, and belongs to all peoples; the second is Christian to those struggling with suffering or victorious over it; the third teaches a spiritual communion of saints —that is to say, of those in the highest degree good and wise. Should not, therefore, the three divine persons under whose symbolism and names such convictions and promises are expressed, be justly held to be in the highest sense a unity?

Religion—Theology.

"I *believe* in God!" that is a fair and a laudable profession; but to *acknowledge* God when and wherever He may reveal Himself, this is the only true blessedness upon earth.

Theism—Theology.

The theological argument for the existence of God has been demolished, it is said, by critical reason; so be it: but what reason fails to prove, feeling, which is equally of divine origin, may be bold to assert. Who can forbid us in the lightning and the thunder and the storm to feel the nearness of an Almighty Power? and in the fragrance of the flowers and the whisperings of the breeze, the loving approaches of a Being who lives in habitual communion with us?

Religion and the Age.

At all times it is the individual that preaches the truth, not the age. It was the age that gave Socrates hemlock for his supper; the age that burnt Huss. The age is always the same.

Aspects of Theological Sentiment.

For myself I honestly confess that, drawn as my soul is in many different directions, I do not feel myself completely satisfied with any one aspect of divine things: as a poet and an artist, I am more or less a polytheist, as a natural philosopher I am a pantheist, and the one neither more nor less than the other; and if I require a personal God for my personality as a moral being, there is provision made in my mental constitution for this also.

Chance.

That which in the enterprises of human beings transcends all calculation, and which is apt to show its power most precisely when human nature is lifting itself most proudly—what men call CHANCE—this is just GOD, who in this incomprehensible way invades our little sphere with His omnipotence, and disturbs our grandest plans, by the intrusion of what to us is a mere accident, but to Him is part of an all-embracing bond.

The Bible.

I am persuaded that the Bible will always appear to us more beautiful, the more it is understood,—that is to say, the more we comprehend that every word in it which we take up in its universal significance, and apply to our own case, had always an immediate and peculiar application connected with the circumstances out of which it arose.

The Bible—Principles of Hermeneutics.

As far back as my twentieth year, I can trace the existence of a certain fundamental conception, or fixed way of viewing things in my mind—whether of native growth or by inoculation from some external source, I cannot say; a conception which I applied to all matters of oral or written tradition. In all such matters, I said to myself, the important thing is the fundamental fact, the internal force, the significance, the tendency; in this alone what is original, divine, operative, unassailable, and indestructible in the tradition, resides; this central and substantial kernel of the matter remains unaffected by any change of condition that time can produce, just as a well-conditioned soul is not disturbed by any accident that may befall the body in which it lies encased. Language, dialect, style, and written tradition are thus to be regarded as the mere body or bearer of a spiritual work; and this body, however closely connected with the internal spirit, is nevertheless subject to deterioration or corruption in many ways; and indeed, in point of fact, it is impossible, in the nature of things, that any tradition should be handed down through long ages quite pure, or, even if it were handed down in perfect purity, that it should be understood through all ages in the same way that it was originally accepted; the former on account of the imperfection of the instruments through which it is handed down, the latter on account of the difference of times and places, and above all, the diversity of human capacities and ways of thinking; a difference which lies at the root of that notable divergence of views which never fails to manifest itself in the schools of antagonistic expositors.

Any person, therefore, who has occasion to occupy himself with the contents of any written tradition, must endeavour to get hold of the marrow of the matter, and that not merely in the way of an intellectual cognition, but in its living relation to his own inner life, and the fruitful action which it produces there; while whatever in the record is of the nature of an external shell, and remains without any moral action upon our souls, or may perhaps even be liable to the suspicion of adulteration, must be thrown aside as of no value for us personally, and left to the disposal of scientific criticism, which, however it may pull in pieces, and tear asunder this part or the other of the whole, can never succeed in robbing us of what we had appropriated in a living way as the root and marrow of the business, or even for a moment making us sceptical as to the fundamental facts which we had sifted out of the kernel of the tradition.

A conviction of this kind, growing out of faith and experimental appropriation, which in all matters of the highest importance is the only effective and operative conviction, lies at the foundation of the moral and literary architecture of my life, and is to be looked upon as a well-invested capital on which a man may richly draw, though, no doubt, in individual cases it may be found wanting. Such a conviction it was that made the Bible in my early years effectively accessible to me. I had read it through several times in the way that is natural to the well-brought-up sons of Protestant parents, and, besides, had plunged into it here and there in a less systematic way, as inclination or edification prompted. The plain-spoken naturalness of the Old Testament, and the tender *naïveté* of the New, had in individual sections taken a strong hold of me; as a whole, no doubt, I was not able to construct it to my satisfaction; but the varieties or apparent contradictions of the different books did one affect my belief in the fundamental conceptions which lay at the root of them all; the significance of each, if not the harmony of the whole, I could fruitfully realise; and, altogether, I had put too much of my best soul into this book to be able ever afterwards to dispense with it as part of my spiritual nourishment. This enlistment of my best feelings on the side of the book made me proof through life against whatever sneers or raillery I might find directed against it; for the spiritual good of which I had been partaker from the book had convinced me experimentally of the dishonesty of all such irreverent assaults. On the other hand, any kind of thorough critical research honestly meant was grateful to me; all extension of our knowledge with regard to oriental localities and costumes I appropriated eagerly, and I employed them without fear in the large and liberal interpretation of the traditions which my spiritual experience had made so dear to me.

With the New Testament I proceeded in the same fearless fashion; but however far, in the exercise of critical ingenuity, I might pull the record to pieces, I always carried with me that most salutary word: "*The Evangelists may contradict themselves as much as they please, so long as the Evangel does not contradict itself.*"

The Bible.

That great homage which the Bible has received from many peoples and from many successive generations it owes to its own intrinsic worth. It is not a book of folk-lore, as other such are found in numbers, but a book for all folk and all peoples, because it takes the fortunes of one people and makes them the symbol of the fortunes of every people, carries back the history of that people to the creation of the world, and 'through a long graduated process of secular and spiritual development and of events partly necessary and partly accidental, carries them forward into the most distant domain of possible eternities.

Two Points of View for the Bible.

There are two points of view from which Biblical matters may be contemplated. The one point is what we may call the standpoint of a sort of primal religion, co-ordinate with the existence of the human species, which point of view is essentially of divine origin. Religion, so considered, is eternally the same, and will remain what it is and was, so long as beings exist in the world capable of knowing divine things; but it is a religion only for a few elect souls, far too high and noble for general reception. The other point of view is that of the CHURCH, which has more of a merely human character; it is never free from a certain weakness, and is always, however imperceptibly, going through a certain process of change; in spite of all which, however, it will persistently remain on the earth, so long as weak human beings inhabit it. The light of undimmed divine revelation is far too pure and too bright to be tolerable to poor weak humanity. The Church steps in as a mediator between the divine fountain of light and the human recipient, and by its mediation so moderates the action of the highest truth as to render it salutary to all, and a source of adequate blessedness to many.

Luther and the Bible.

Luther sees in the Old and New Testaments the symbol of the great cosmic Being, who in His manifestation is ever repeating Himself in diverse forms. In the Old Testament he sees Law, which strives after its consummation in Love; in the New he sees Love, which asserts itself against Law, which it at the same time fulfils by planting it on a higher platform —not, however, by any power or virtue residing in the individual, but by faith, and that an exclusive faith, in the all-revealing and all-working Messiah. This single point will be enough to let us see how Lutheranism never can come to any agreement with Popery, while on the other hand there is nothing in it that should lead it to refuse an alliance with pure reason, so soon as pure reason consents to look on the Bible as a mirror of the moral history of the world—a feat which it should not in any wise be difficult for pure reason to achieve.

Bible Societies.

People have quarrelled and will quarrel much about the advantage or disadvantage of promiscuous Bible circulation. To me it is quite clear that the Bible will continue to do harm, as it has hitherto done, when used in the interest of scholastic dogma or fantastic mysticism; while it will continue to do good in the future, as it has done in the past, wherever the element of moral purity and devout sentiment is dominant in its treatment.

True Religion.

Religion, most properly so called, is always a matter of the inner man, and a thing specially belonging to the individual; for it has to do directly with the conscience, at one time to rouse it from lethargy, at another time to soothe it when fretted. For the conscience in any breast may exist in a numbed, dull, and ineffective state; on a person suffering under such a moral cachexy, religion acts as a stimulant: or again, the consciousness of sin, with remorseful unrest accompanying the same, may become so intense as to embitter existence: here religion steps in as a balm.

Christianity.

The Christian religion is a mighty lever, by the help of which degraded and suffering humanity has again and again been strengthened to lift itself out of the mire; and by allowing it the possession of this great moral efficiency, we place it on a platform higher than all philosophy, and where, indeed, for the manifestation of its highest virtue no philosophy is required.

Corruption of Christianity.

Shortly after its promulgation, Christianity suffered from an invasion of subtle and senseless heresies, whereby it lost its original purity. Further on, when it attempted to control and to mould altogether rude and morally degraded peoples, drastic measures were necessary; and then, not teaching so much as liturgical services and ceremonials, came into play. For converts of such rude type the one mediator, whom we all know, between God in heaven and earthly man, was not sufficient; and in this way arose that strange compound of heathenism and Hebraism, which, under the name of Christianity, has asserted itself through the centuries with notable display.

Luther.

It is difficult for us fully to realise how much we owe to Luther and the Reformation, not only in the

Church, but as human beings and members of human society. We have been emancipated from the fetters of intellectual limitation; and as a consequence of our progressive culture, starting from the point of his Protest, we have become capable of going back to the fountain-head, and reaching Christianity in its original purity. We have the courage again to stand with firm foot upon God's earth, and to feel our dignity as reasonable creatures inheriting glorious gifts from God. Let intellectual culture mount as high as it may, let the natural sciences expand and extend to an indefinite amount, and let the mind of man career freely in the widest conceivable range—at no stage of human progress is it possible that humanity should rise above, and plant itself beyond, the light and ethical culture of Christianity, as it shines forth and radiates with unsullied splendour in the Gospels.

And the more thoroughly and earnestly we Protestants advance to the practical comprehension of this pure evangelic Christianity, the more quickly will the Catholics follow in our track, till at length it will come about that Protestants and Catholics meet in a common form of Christianity, redeemed from all adventitious impurities. Then also the wretched petty sectarian activity into which Protestantism has shown a tendency to resolve itself will cease, and between father, son, sister and mother, natural love, not unnatural hatred, will prevail. And all of us by degrees will learn to elevate ourselves out of a Chris-

tianity of catechisms and creeds, into a Christianity
of pure sentiment and noble action.

Abuse of the Divine Name.

People treat the divine name as if that incomprehensible and most high Being, who is even beyond the reach of thought, were only their equal. Otherwise, they would not say the *Lord God*, the *dear God*, the *good God*. This expression becomes to them, especially to the clergy, who have it daily in their mouths, a mere phrase, a barren name, to which no thought is attached whatever. If they were truly impressed by His greatness they would be dumb, and through veneration unwilling to name Him.

Honesty and Orthodoxy.

In religious, scientific, and political matters, I generally brought trouble upon myself, because I was no hypocrite, and had the courage to express what I felt.

I believed in God and in Nature, and in the triumph of good over evil; but this was not enough for the godly people: I was required to believe other points, which were opposed to the feeling of my soul for truth; besides, I did not see how these notions could be of the slightest service to me.

Immortality.

Man is entitled to believe in immortality; such belief is agreeable to his nature; and his instincts in this direction are confirmed by religious assurances. My belief in the immortality of the soul springs from the idea of activity; for when I persevere to the end in a course of restless activity, I have a sort of guarantee from Nature that, when the present form of my existence proves itself inadequate for the energising of my spirit, she will provide another form more appropriate.

When a man is seventy-five years old, he cannot avoid now and then thinking of death. This thought, when it comes, leaves me in a state of perfect peace, for I have the most assured conviction that our soul is of an essence absolutely indestructible; an essence that works on from eternity to eternity. It is like the sun, which to our earthly eyes sinks and sets, but in reality never sinks, but shines on unceasingly.

Immortality and Tiedge.

I have had to endure not a little from Tiedge's 'Urania;' for, at one time, nothing was sung and nothing was declaimed but this same 'Urania.' Wherever you went, you found 'Urania' on the table. 'Urania' and immortality were the topics of every conversation. I would by no means dispense with the happiness of believing in a future existence, and, indeed, would say, with Lorenzo de Medici, that those are dead even for this life who hope for no other. But such incomprehensible matters lie too far off to be a theme of daily meditation and thought-distracting speculation. Let him who believes in immortality enjoy his happiness in silence, he has no reason to give himself airs about it. The occasion of Tiedge's 'Urania' led me to observe that piety, like nobility, has its aristocracy. I met stupid women, who plumed themselves on believing, with Tiedge, in immortality, and I was forced to bear much dark examination on this point. They were vexed by my saying I should be well pleased if, after the close of this life, we were blessed with another, only I hoped I should hereafter meet none of those who had believed in it here. For how should I be tormented! The godly people would throng around me, and say, Were we not right? Did we not predict it? Has not it happened just as we said? And so there would be *ennui* without end even in the other world.

This occupation with the idea of immortality is for people of rank, and especially ladies, who have nothing to do. But an able man, who has something regular to do here, and must toil and struggle and produce day by day, leaves the future world to itself, and is active and useful in this. Thoughts about immortality are also good for those who have not been very successful here; and I would wager that, if the good Tiedge had enjoyed a better lot, he would also have had better thoughts.

Religion of Daily Life:

Some persons, who throughout the whole twelve months are worldly, think it necessary to be godly at a time of straits; all moral and religious matters they regard as physic, which is to be taken, with aversion, when they are unwell. In a clergyman, a moralist, they see nothing but a doctor, whom they cannot soon enough get rid of. Now, I confess, I look upon religion as a kind of diet, which can be so only when I make a constant practice of it,—when throughout the whole twelve months I never lose sight of it.

Religion and Books.

The use of books, catechisms, sermons, and even the Bible itself, in all the deeper matters of religion, is secondary. The man to whom the universe does not reveal directly what relation it has to him,— whose heart does not tell him what he owes himself and others,—that man will scarcely learn it out of books, which generally do little more than give our errors names.

Animal Instincts and God.

There is in the curious and kindly operation of animal instincts something which, whosoever studies and does not believe in God, will not be aided by Moses and the prophets. In these instincts I perceive what I call the omnipresence of the Deity, who has everywhere spread and implanted a portion of His endless love, and has intimated, even in the brute, as a germ those qualities which blossom to perfection in the noblest forms of man.

Religion and Superstition.

A tendency to superstition is of the very essence of humanity; and, when we think we have completely extinguished it, we shall find it retreating into the strangest nooks and corners, that it may issue out thence on the first occasion it can do so with safety.

Spiritualism, Presentiments, Dreams, &c.

Of all the superstitions which infest the brains of weak mortals, the belief in prophecies, presentiments, and dreams, seems to me amongst the most pitiful and pernicious. By the traffic in such fancies no doubt a certain fictitious significance is given to the common events of daily life, in quiet times; but when in great epochs life becomes fraught with seriousness, and a real significance, when the storms of change are roaring and buffeting around us, then the belief in those phantoms of feeble brains only makes the commotion more terrible.

Time and Eternity.

I am heartily sorry for those persons who are constantly talking of the perishable nature of things, and the nothingness of human life; for, for this very end we are here, to stamp the perishable with an imperishable worth; and this can be done only by taking a just estimate of both.

Religion and Metaphysics.

Man is not born to solve the problems of the universe, but to find out where the problem begins, and then to restrain himself within the limits of the comprehensible. His faculties are not sufficient to measure the activities of the universe; and an attempt to explain the outer world by reason, from his narrow point of view, is a vain endeavour. The reason of man and the reason of the Deity are two very different things. If we grant freedom to man, there is an end to the omniscience of God; for, if the Divinity knows how I shall act, I must act so, perforce. I give this merely as a sign how little we know, and to show that it is not good to meddle with divine mysteries. Moreover, we should only give utterance to the highest truths so far as it can benefit the world. What lies beyond the common appetite and the common power of appropriation we should keep within ourselves, and it will diffuse over our actions a lustre like the mild radiance of a hidden sun.

Religion.

Religion is not an end, but a means whereby to reach the highest culture through the greatest peace of soul.

There are only two true religions: one which recognises and adores the Holy in us and around us, unclothed with any special form; and another, which recognises and worships it in the most beautiful form. All intermediate religions are forms of idol-worship.

Religion and Good Works.

So soon as good works, and their merit before God, were put out of view by the Protestants, pious sentiment and superfine sentimentalism came in to supply their place. Men must have something to pride themselves on.

Prayer and Providence.

As we do know a king by overflow
Of largesses—for what to him is little
Were wealth to thousands; so we know your grace,
Ye mighty gods, by bounties long prepared
And wisely stored to serve man's needful hour;
For only you know what is good for man,

Before whose eyes the wide extended realm
Of the far future open lies, while we
With every peeping star and evening mist
Find our view shortened. With wise patience ye
List to our prayers that with childish fret
Cry out for instant answer; but your hand
Breaks not the branch that bears the golden fruit
With bounty premature; and woe to him
In your despite who plucks the unripe grace
With hasty hand, and feeds on bitter food
Till he may die!

God and Humanity.

The good gods love the good and widely spread
Races of mortal kind, well pleased to stretch
His little term to man, and lend to him
For a short season, with a liberal grace,
The fellow-vision and the joy with them
Of their own deathless being in the sky.

Wisdom—Human and Divine.

Vain is all human wisdom, if the wise
Lend not their ears to list the will divine.
Upon some noble soul that grossly sinned,
Some god hath laid a sore atoning task
That seems to mock all strength of man, when lo!
The hero conquers, and with one sure stroke
Devoutly serves the faithful-helping gods,
And the admiring world.

Two Faces of Providence.

The gods who in their blazing potency
With fulminant volleys charge the weighty clouds,
And sternly kind the long-expected rain
With thunder voice and whirl of warring winds
Fling out in wild floods o'er the thirsty earth;
They into blessing change the bane anon;
And men that quaked with fearful expectation
Transform to joyful looks, soon as the new
Outbursting sun is seen a thousand times
Glassed in the dew-drops of the freshened leaves,
While purple Iris parts with friendly touch
The thin-wove tissue of the last grey cloud.

Religion—God—Sacrifice.

The gods are good, and do not thirst for blood;
Who calls them vengeful but transfers the type
Of his own earthly nature into heaven,
And stamps them human.

Religion—Life.

The gods need many a noble man to do
Their work on earth. They count on me and you.

Duties to God and Man.

Men live on easy terms with God; and why?
Because aloft far in the topmost sky
    He holds His sway,
And never comes, as men do, in their way.

God.

No! such a God my worship may not win,
Who lets the world about His finger spin,
A thing extern : my God must rule within,
And whom I own for Father, God, Creator,
Holds nature in Himself, Himself in nature ;
And in His kindly arms embraced, the Whole
Doth live and move by His pervading soul.

The Divine Procedure.

How?—when?—and where?—the gods give no reply;
What they will do, they do : nor heed your Why?

God—Innate Ideas.

There is a universe within,
The world we call the soul, the mind :
And in that world what best we find
We stammer forth, and think no sin
To call it God, and our God, and
Give heaven and earth into His hand,
And fear His power, and search His plan
Darkly, and love Him, when we can.

The Infinite.

Wouldst thou with thy bounded sight
Make survey of the Infinite,
Look right and left, and everywhere,
Into the finite—you'll find it there.

Toleration.

The *Pater noster* is a goodly prayer,
That helped poor sinners out of many a scrape:
And if one prays it a *noster Pater*,
Well, let it help him in that shape!

Divine and Human.

What men would wish to have is felt below;
What should be given to men is known above.
We teem with mighty projects; but to lead
Up to the ever good and ever fair,
Is the gods' work; leave to the gods their own.

Nature and Grace.

I wander here in Nature's garden fair,
And pick up blooms of beauty here and there,
And in this garden find a well of grace,
And old tradition that makes glad the place.

Self-knowledge and Knowledge of God.

Wouldst know thyself, and not acknowledge God?
Who begins thus may end in worshipping a clod.

Religion and Morality.

Who lifts his thought to God will never sink
Far 'neath the level of what he dares to think.

The New Birth.

Die to the old; live to the new;
Grow strong with each to-morrow:
Else drag with thee to life's dull end,
A lengthening chain of sorrow!

Gloomy Imaginations—Despondency.

Death's bad enough, and black enough in faith;
But why paint life in funeral hues of Death?

Immortality.

A rescued spirit to the goal
    We bring of earth's probation;
The ever-active stirring soul
    Works out its own salvation.
And, when in love and mercy strong,
    His God and Saviour meets him,
The angel-choir to join their throng,
    With hearty welcome greets him.

Hymn of the Angels.

RAPHAEL.

The sun doth chime his ancient music,
'Mid brothered spheres' contending song,
And on his fore-appointed journey,
With pace of thunder rolls along.

Strength drink the angels from his glory,
Though none may throughly search his way:
God's works rehearse their wondrous story,
As bright as on Creation's day.

GABRIEL.

And swift and swift beyond conceiving,
The pomp of earth is wheeled around.
Alternating Elysian brightness
With awful gloom of night profound.
Up foams the sea, a surging river,
And smites the steep rock's echoing base,
And rock and sea, unwearied ever,
Spin their eternal circling race.

MICHAEL.

And storm meets storm with rival greeting
From sea to land, from land to sea;
While from their war a virtue floweth,
That thrills with life all things that be.
The lightning darts his fury, blazing
Before the thunder's sounding way;
But still Thy servants, Lord, are praising
The gentle going of Thy day.

ALL THE THREE.

Strength drink the angels from Thy glory,
Though none may search Thy wondrous way
Thy works repeat their radiant story,
As bright as on Creation's day.

The Prophet.

Not the Future alone; the Past is the realm of the
  prophet;
Often, how often their Past reads like a riddle to
  men!
Whoso knows the Past may divine the Future: the
  Present
Binds with a perfecting bond link unto link of the
  years.

Good and Evil: their action and issue
(loquitur Dominus Deus).

Of all the spirits that deny,
  The clever rogue sins least against my mind.
For, in good sooth, the mortal generation,
  When a soft pillow they may haply find,
Are far too apt to sink into stagnation;
And therefore, man for comrade wisely gets
A devil, who spurs, and stimulates, and whets.
But you, ye sons of heaven's own choice,
In the one living Beautiful rejoice!
The self-evolving energy divine
Enclasp you round with love's embrace benign,
And on the floating forms of earth and sky,
Stamp the fair type of thought that may not die!

God in Everything.

1.

The East belongs to God; the West
Gladly obeys His high behest;
Tropic heat, and Arctic cold,
His hand in peaceful bond doth hold.

2.

Only God is just; He sees
  What is good for each and all:
Call Him by what name you please,
  But praise His name, both great and small.

3.

Life's a labyrinth, whose plan
Thou canst not learn from wit of man;
But make God guide in all thy ways,
And He will lead thee through the maze.

4.

Two graces give our breathing worth,
To draw air in, then send it forth;
That with a power to cramp and tighten,
This to expand us, and to lighten;—
So wondrously our life unites
Mysterious play of opposites.
Then thank thou God when He confines thy way,
And thank Him too when He gives larger sway.

The Bible.

Even as that maid of saintly grace
Took to herself the Saviour's face
In her white kerchief, so I took
Into my soul the holy Book,
And there in spite of sceptic error,
Gloomy doubt, and fearful terror,
I kept unharmed from cloudy scath
The pure bright image of the faith.

Bright and Brightest.

Bright is the fair maid's eye that looks on thine;
Bright is the drinker's eye that greets the wine;
And like the sun that robes the flowery year,
The sovereign's word falls on the favoured ear.
But brighter far than all these bright-faced things
Are the fair thanks thy gracious bounty brings
From the poor starveling, that with beaming face
And outspread hand receives thy kindly grace:
Peruse it well, that speaking face, and thou
Wilt ever give, as thou art giving now.

Quiet Working.

Ask not by what gate thou entered
  Into life, the garden of God;
But in the quiet nook assigned thee,
  Trim the beds and break the clod.

Look around thee, then, for wise men,
  Look for men of high command;
These will help thee with good counsel,
  These will give strength to thy hand.

And when long years of faithful service
  Thou hast given to the State,
Know that many then will love thee,
  Know that none will dare to hate.

And the prince will own the loyal
  Soul, that breathes through all thy ways,
Linking firmly each to-morrow
  With long chain of yesterdays.

Charity.

Jesus, as He walked through the world,
  To a fleshmarket came one day,
And there before the butcher's door
  Right on the road a dead dog lay.
A crowd around the carcass stood,
  As vultures gather; and one said,
"The stench of this abhorrèd hound
  Sickens my brain inside my head."
Another said, "The grave has cast
  Its refuse up for bad luck here;"
And thus each in his way reproached
  The poor dead brute with bitter jeer.

Then the Lord Jesus oped His mouth—
  Not He with sharp reproach and spite;
But from a loving heart and true,
  He said, " Like pearls his teeth are white."
They heard, and none might dare to blame;
  Their hearts were burning hot with shame.

Toleration.

If God to men were as severe
  As you and I are, when we jar,
We both had scanty comfort here;
  But He takes men just as they are.

Stupid Piety.

If the Ass whose back did carry,
'Mid pomp of palms, the Son of Mary,
To Mecca should devoutly fare,
And worship with the pilgrims there,
He would go and back return
An ass—the ass that he was born!

The Four Gospels.

Jesus came down from heaven, and brought
The text of the gospels in His hand,—
The text which God's own finger wrote,—
And read it to the faithful band
Of His disciples. The word of grace
Once sown in good soil grows apace.

He rose to heaven, and with him took
The faultless text of the sacred book;
But in their hearts the truth remained,
And each one wrote from day to day
What in his memory each retained,
And pictured forth in his own way.
Well, they were men, to whom God lent
A diverse wit, and diverse bent,
And therewith we must be content:
We'll get no more, one thing is clear,
Till the last trump sounds in our ear.

Admission.

HOURI.

Here by Heaven's decree I stand,
    A warder at the gate of grace;
Thou wouldst come in, but strange misgiving
    Stirs me when I read thy face.

Art thou faithful to the prophet?
    Of our cousinship and kin?
Through what sweatful struggle didst thou
    Earn the right to enter in?

Didst thou draw thy sword for Allah?
    Show thy wounds and claim reward:
Never yet against the faithful
    Was the blissful portal barred.

POET.

Why this doubting and misgiving?
    I'm a man; be this enough.
Life's a battle; I have fought it
    With sharp sword and temper tough.

Whet thine eyes, and look within me,
    See the wounds that scar this heart,
Wounds from Fortune's freakish humour,
    Wounds from Love's delicious dart!

Yet my faith was never shaken:
    I believed my love was true;
Never cursed the babbling world,
    Though it gave me much ado.

With a band of noble workers
    I did work, and knew no rest,
Till my name woke love bright-flaming
    From the hearts of all the best.

No, thou wilt not choose the worser;
    Give thy hand, and grant me this,
To live, and on thy dainty fingers
    Count eternities of bliss.[1]

---

[1] This poem is from the 'West-Eastern Divan,' a work in which the great German pleased to identify himself with Hafiz, the Persian poet. This will explain the Mohammedan character of the celestial warders.

POLITICS

Willst Du viele befreyen, so wag es vielen zu dienen;
Wie gefährlich das sey, willst Du es wissen, versuch's.

POLITICS.

Reform, Revolution, and Conservatism.

It is true that I could be no friend to the French Revolution; for its horrors were too near me, and shocked me daily and hourly, whilst its beneficial results were not then to be discovered. Neither could I be indifferent to the fact that the Germans were endeavouring artificially to bring about such scenes here, as were in France the consequence of a great necessity. But I was as little a friend to arbitrary rule. Indeed I was perfectly convinced that a great revolution is never a fault of the people, but of the government. Revolutions are utterly impossible, as long as governments are constantly just and constantly vigilant; so that they may anticipate them by improvements at the right time, and not hold out until they are forced to yield by the pressure from beneath. Because I hated the Revolution, the name of "the friend of the powers that be" was bestowed upon me. That is, however, a very ambiguous title, which I would beg to decline. If "the powers that be" were all that is excellent, good, and just, I should have no objection to the title; but, since with much that is good there is also much that is bad, unjust, and imperfect, a friend of "the things that are" means often little less than a friend of the obsolete and bad. But time is constantly progressing, and human affairs wear every fifty years a different aspect; so that an arrangement which, in the year 1800, was perfection, may, perhaps, in the year 1850, be a defect. And furthermore, nothing is good for a nation but that which arises from its own case and its own special wants, without apish imitation of another; since what to one race of people, of a certain age, is a wholesome nutriment, may perhaps prove a poison for another. All endeavours, therefore, to introduce any foreign innovation, the necessity for which is not rooted in the core of the nation itself, are foolish; and all premeditated revolutions of the kind are unsuccessful, for they are without God, who keeps aloof from such bungling. If, however, there exists an actual necessity for a great reform amongst a people, God is with it, and it prospers. He was visibly with Christ and His first adherents; for the appearance of the new doctrine of love was a necessity to the people. He was also visibly with Luther; for the purification of the doctrine corrupted by the priests was no less a necessity.

Neither of the great powers whom I have named was conservative of the state of things that then existed; much rather were both of them convinced that the old leaven must be got rid of, and that it would be impossible to go on and remain in the untrue, unjust, and defective way.

Government.

In the government of men a great deal may be done by severity, more by love, but most of all by clear discernment and impartial justice which pays no respect to persons.

Revolutions.

I hate every violent overthrow, because as much is destroyed as is gained by it. I hate those who achieve it, as well as those who give cause for it. But am I therefore no friend to the public? Does any right-minded man think otherwise?

You know how greatly I rejoice at every improvement of which the future gives us some prospect. But, as I said, all violent transitions are revolting to my mind, for they are not conformable to nature.

I am a friend to plants; I love the rose, as the most perfect flower which our German soil can produce; but I am not fool enough to desire that my garden should produce them now, at the end of April.

I am satisfied if I now find the first green leaves—satisfied if I see how one leaf after another is formed upon the stem, from week to week; I am pleased when, in May, I perceive the buds; and I am happy when, at last, in June, the rose itself appears in all its splendour, and all its fragrance. If any one cannot wait, let him go to the hothouses.

Aristocracy—Nobility—Pedigree—Primogeniture— Entail.

If the State, for a regular and fair contribution, would relieve us from the feudal hocus-pocus—would allow us to deal with our lands according to our pleasure, so that we were not compelled to retain such masses of them undivided—in that case we might introduce our children to a course of vigorous and free activity, instead of leaving them the poor inheritance of these our limited and limiting privileges, to enjoy which we must ever be invoking the spirits of our fathers. How much happier were men and women in our rank of life, if they might with unforbidden eyes look round them, and elevate by their selection, here a worthy maiden, there a worthy youth, regarding nothing farther than their own ideas of happiness in marriage! The State would have more, perhaps better citizens, and would not so often be distressed for want of heads and hands.

Aristocracy and Democracy.

Much is said of Aristocracy and Democracy, but the whole affair is simply this: in youth, when we possess nothing, or know not how to value tranquil possessions, we are democrats; but when in a long life we have acquired property, we wish not only to be secure of it ourselves, but also that our children and grandchildren shall be secure of inheriting it, and quietly enjoying it. Therefore, in old age, we are always aristocrats, to whatever opinions we may have been inclined in youth.

Freedom—Schiller.

Freedom is an odd thing, and every man has enough of it, if he can only satisfy himself. What avails a superfluity of freedom which we cannot use? Look at this chamber and the next, in which, through the open door, you see my bed. Neither of them is large; and they are rendered still narrower by necessary furniture, books, manuscripts, and works of art; but they are enough for me. I have lived in them all the winter, scarcely entering my front rooms. What have I done with my spacious house, and the liberty of going from one room to another, when I have not found it requisite to make use of them?

If a man has freedom enough to live healthily, and work at his craft, he has enough; and so much all can easily obtain. Then all of us are only free under certain conditions, which we must fulfil. The citizen is as free as the nobleman, when he restrains himself within the limits which God appointed by placing him in that rank. The nobleman is as free as the prince, for, if he will but observe a few ceremonies at court, he may feel himself his equal. Freedom consists not in refusing to recognise anything above us, but in respecting something which is above us; for, by respecting it, we raise ourselves to it, and by our very acknowledgment make manifest that we bear within ourselves what is higher, and are worthy to be on a level with it.

I have, on my journeys, often met merchants from the north of Germany, who fancied they were my equals, if they rudely seated themselves next me at table. They were, by this method, nothing of the kind; but they would have been so, if they had known how to value and treat me.

That this physical freedom gave Schiller so much trouble in his youthful years, was caused partly by the nature of his mind, but still more by the restraint which he endured at the military school. In later days, when he had enough physical freedom, he passed over to the idea; and I would almost say that the idea killed him, since it led him to make demands on his physical nature which were too much for his strength.

Democracy—Majorities.

Nothing is more abhorrent to a reasonable man than an appeal to a majority; for it consists of a few strong men, as leaders, of knaves who temporise, of the feeble who are hangers-on, and of the multitudes who follow without the slightest idea of what they want.

Command and Obedience.

He alone is happy who requires neither to command nor obey, in order to be something in the world.

Weak Characters and Politics.

Weak characters are apt to make a law of their weakness. A man who knew the world well said, "Nothing is more difficult to contend with than prudence, under which fear shields itself." Weak men have often revolutionary sentiments; they imagine it would go well with them, if they were not forced to obey a government, not knowing that they must be governed, simply because they are too weak to govern either themselves or others.

Civilisation.

There is something more or less wrong among us old Europeans; our relations are far too artificial and complicated; our nutriment and mode of life are without their proper nature; and our social intercourse is without proper love and goodwill. Every one is polished and courteous; but no one has the courage to be hearty and true, so that an honest man, with natural views and feelings, stands in a very bad position. Often one cannot help wishing that one had been born upon one of the South Sea Islands, a so-called savage, so as to have thoroughly enjoyed human existence in all its purity, without any adulteration.

Government.

The world is governed by wisdom, by authority, and by show.

Courts and Courtiers.

Court life is like music, in which every one must keep time.

Courtiers would die of *ennui*, if they could not fill up their time with ceremonies.

Action and Reaction.

The battle between the old and the new, the persistent and the progressive, is always the same. All order is apt to stiffen into a lifeless formalism; to get rid of which, order is destroyed, and some time will elapse before people see that order must be recalled. Classicism and romanticism, monopolies of guilds and freedom of crafts, accumulation and division of land,—under whatever name, it is always the same conflict, which, after fighting out its result in one direction, in due season creates a new conflict in the opposite direction. The great wisdom of governments would be so to regulate this conflict, that a balance might be established betwixt the two opposites, creating the new without the absolute loss of the old; but this is something that seems to go beyond the strength of men, and God, so far as we may judge, does not seem to wish it.[1]

Freedom.

The moment men obtain perfect freedom, that moment they erect a stage for the manifestation of their faults. The strong characters begin to go wrong by excess of energy; the weak by remissness in action.

Revolutionary Times.

Oh, these are times of dread significance!
Times when the low man mounts, the lofty falls,

---

[1] This seems to be generalised from the history of the French Revolution. We English flatter ourselves, sometimes, that we are masters in the art of reform without revolution. But we also had our Civil War, our Commonwealth, and our Restoration; and no man knows what may yet be awaiting us.—J. S. B.

As each man only in his neighbour's place
Could find the food to feed his vague desire,
Then only live a happy hour, when all
Distinctions vanish, and all we love is borne
In one huge stream of motley huddlement
Into the vast and indiscriminate swell
Of the wide ocean.

Ancestry and Aristocracy—Heredity.

Happy who with a bright regard looks back
Upon his father's fathers, who with joy
Recounts their deeds of grace, and in himself
Values the latest link in the fair chain
Of noble sequences; for Nature loves
Not at one bound to achieve her topmost type,
But step by step she leads a family on
To demigod or devil, the rare joy
Or horror of the world.

Freedom.

Man was not born to say—*I will be free;*
No higher good a noble man may wish,
Than with a loyal heart to serve a prince
Whom he respects and honours.

Obedience.

A noble master all may well obey
Whose word convinces, where his will commands.

The Many.

Trust not the many : they stare at your mishap,
Doubt, and delay, and leave you where you were ;
No fair design to fruitful end may grow
From fancies lightly stirred, and blindly led.

The Demos.

To οἱ πολλοί I would be civil ;
When things go smoothly, they do well ;
But, when the storm blows fierce and fell,
Then they, to exorcise the devil,
Bring up a host of knaves pell-mell,
With tyrants on their back from hell.

The French Revolution.

Mad are those Frenchmen you say, those flaming apostles of freedom,
Flinging the torch of revolt wildly far east and far west :
Mad I agree; but freemen ofttimes with their madness will mingle
Words of wisdom ; the slave, wise man or fool, must be dumb !

All apostles of freedom I hate, and hated them ever ;
Lawless licence they seek, each for himself in the end.

Wouldst thou give freedom to many, first dare to do
    service to many;
Dangerous daring! and yet this you may learn, if
    you try!

France and her caldron of troubles, the great of the
    earth may consider;
More than the great the small wisely the lesson may
    read.
Nemesis seized the few; but who will deliver the
    many
From the many, when they brook many tyrants for
    one?

LITERATURE—POETRY

Was macht den Dichter?—Ein volles, ganz von einer edlen
Empfindung volles Herz.

LITERATURE—POETRY.

Poetry and Popular Life : The Greeks—Burns.

WE admire the TRAGEDIES of the ancient GREEKS; but to take a correct view of the case, we ought to admire the period and the nation in which their production was possible rather than the individual authors; for though these pieces differ in some points from each other, and though one of these poets appears somewhat greater and more finished than the other, still, taking all things together, only one decided character runs through the whole.

This is the character of grandeur, fitness, soundness, human perfection, elevated wisdom, sublime thought, pure strong intuition, and whatever other qualities one might enumerate. But when we find all these qualities, not only in the dramatic works which have come down to us, but also in lyrical and epic works — in the philosophers, orators, and historians, and in an equally high degree in the works of plastic art that have come down to us—we must feel convinced that such qualities did not merely belong to individuals, but were the current property of the nation and the whole period.

Now, take up BURNS. How is he great, except through the circumstance that the whole songs of his predecessors lived in the mouth of the people,—that they were, so to speak, sung at his cradle; that, as a boy, he grew up amongst them; and the high excellence of these models so pervaded him that he had therein a living basis on which he could proceed further? Again, why is he great, but from this, that his own songs at once found susceptible ears amongst his compatriots; that, sung by reapers and sheaf-binders, they at once greeted him in the field; and that his boon-companions sang them to welcome him at the ale-house?

Novelty.

POETRY operates most strongly in the beginning of new social conditions—it may be when the people is quite crude, half cultivated, or in the transition from one stage of social culture to another, or on the discovery of a foreign culture; but in all these cases NOVELTY acts as the most potent stimulus in producing the result.[1]

---

[1] It may be worth while noticing that in the few books on taste published in the last century, it was a common thing to place *novelty* in the van, as if this were the most important principle to be considered in an æsthetical treatise. This was to confound

The Novel and the Drama.

In the novel as well as in the drama, it is human nature and human action that we see. The difference between these casts of fiction lies not merely in their outward form—not merely in the circumstance that the personages of the one are made to speak, whilst those of the other have commonly their history narrated. Unfortunately, many dramas are but novels, which proceed by dialogue, and it would not be impossible to write a drama in the shape of letters. But in the novel it is chiefly sentiments and events that are exhibited; in the drama it is characters and deeds. The novel must go slowly forward, and the sentiments of the hero, by some means or another, must restrain the tendency of the whole to unfold itself and to conclude. The drama, on the other hand, must hasten, and the character of the hero must press forward to the end; it does not restrain but is restrained. The novel hero must be suffering—at least he must not be in a high degree active; in the dramatic hero we look for activity and deeds. Grandison, Clarissa, Pamela, the Vicar of Wakefield, Tom Jones himself, were, if not suffering, at least retarding personages. And the incidents are all, in some sort, modelled by their sentiments. In the

an external exciting occasion with an inward plastic cause, in a manner not at all creditable to the philosophical endowment of the century.—J. S. B.

drama the hero models nothing by himself; all things withstand him, and he clears and casts away the hindrances from off his path, or else sinks under them.

In the novel some degree of scope may be allowed to chance, but it must always be led and guided by the sentiments of the personages; on the other hand, Fate, which by means of connected circumstances carries forward men without their own concurrence to an unforeseen catastrophe, can have place only in the drama; Chance may produce pathetic situations, but never tragic ones. Fate, on the other hand, ought always to be terrible, and is in the highest sense tragic, when it brings into a close concatenation the guilty man and the guiltless confounded in one sweeping doom.

Milton.

The other day (1799) I happened to take up Milton's 'Paradise Lost,' which threw me into strange contemplations. In this, as in all other productions of modern art, it is the personality of the artist that gives interest to his work. The subject is detestable (*abschenlich*); externally not without a certain imposing grandeur, but internally worm-eaten and hollow. The springs of action, and the situations that belong to them—*die motiven*—are in some few cases natural and effective; but the majority are lame and false, and give one pain to realise. At the same time, it is an interesting man who speaks to us: character, feeling, understanding, learning, poetical and oratorical genius, and other excellent qualities, he undoubtedly possesses in no common measure. Nay, more; the singular accident that as a revolutionary politician he paints the devil with more effective touches than the angels, has a great influence on the design and composition of the poem; and again, the accident of the writer being blind, adds not a little to the tone and colour of the book. 'Paradise Lost,' therefore, notwithstanding its radical defects as a work of art, will maintain its place triumphantly in virtue of the majestic personality (*Natur*) which it reveals.

Books.

Properly speaking, we learn from those books only that we cannot judge. The author of a book that I am competent to criticise would have to learn from me.

Excellence and Mediocrity.

All great excellence in life or art, at its first recognition, brings with it a certain pain arising from the strongly felt inferiority of the spectator; only at a later period, when we take it into our own culture, and appropriate as much of it as our capacities allow, we learn to love and to esteem it. Mediocrity on the other hand may often give us unqualified pleasure; it does not disturb our self-satisfaction, but rather encourages us with the thought that we are as good as another.

Books.

Books also have their strange living experiences.

> *Who ne'er his bread with weeping ate,*
> *And through night's sorrow-laden hours,*
> *Weeping on bed of languor sate,*
> *He knows you not, ye heavenly Powers!*[1]

These deeply pathetic lines were frequently repeated by a noble and much-revered queen in her banishment. She formed acquaintance with the book in which the lines occur—a book in which not a few other sorrowful experiences are recorded—and drew from the perusal a painful consolation. Influences of this kind may proceed even from inferior books, and give a pulsation of good continued through eternity; and who could grudge or seek to curtail good results of this nature?

Advice to Young Poets.

Let the young poet give utterance only to what lives, and lives not for the moment, let its form be

---

[1] Well-known lines from 'Wilhelm Meister:' the royal lady alluded to is the Louise, Queen of Prussia, whom Napoleon treated so rudely.—J. S. B.

what it will; above all, let him have nothing to do with anything in the shape of ill-humour or contradiction or negation; from saying No, however cleverly, no good can come.

It is of great consequence to grow in rhythmical dexterity and execution, but all this will be of no avail, if a constant eye be not kept on the solidity and substantiality of the contents. Now poetical contents, or what the wine merchants call *body*, mean always fundamentally the contents of the author's own life which nobody can give us, and nobody can take from us. Happily in the present day all products of mere vanity and self-display, with no root, meet with less favour than ever.

I cannot prescribe any form to be followed—you must make your own form; only in the case of every poem, ask if it contains a real experience, and if it be an experience by which your own higher life has been benefited. You are not benefited, for instance, when you go on continually lamenting for some loved one that you have lost through distance, infidelity, or death. However cleverly you put forth wailings of this sort, you are nothing the better for it. Keep yourselves always in the forward march of life, and free yourself as you go along.

Poetry and Misanthropy.

A well-known German poet had lately passed through Weimar, and shown Goethe his album. You cannot imagine, said Goethe, what stuff it contains. All the poets write as if they were ill, and the whole world were a lazaretto. They all speak of the woe and the misery of this earth, and of the joys of a hereafter; all are discontented, and one draws the other into a state of still greater discontent. This is a real abuse of poetry, which was given to us to hide the little discords of life, and to make man contented with the world and his condition. But the present generation is afraid of all such strength, and only feels poetical when it has weakness to deal with.

I have hit on a good word to tease these gentlemen. I will call their poetry "Lazaretto-poetry;" and I will give the name of "Tyrtæan-poetry" to that which not only sings war-songs, but also arms men with courage to undergo the conflicts of life.

Our Young Poets.

The majority of our young poets have no fault but this, that their subjectivity is not important, and that they cannot find matter in the objective. At best they only find a material which is similar to themselves, which corresponds to their own subjectivity; but as for taking the material on its own account, when it is repugnant to their subjectivity, merely because it is poetical, such a thing is never thought of.

Poetry; Subjective and Objective.

The province of the poet is representation. Representation becomes more perfect the more closely it vies with nature, when the pictures through the genius of the poet are so vivid that they work on mind with all the force of realities. Poetry is at its zenith when it seems altogether external; the more it deals with the personal feeling of the writer, the more it is on the downward path. That poetry which describes only the feelings of the writer, without giving them an outward body, and on the other hand that which gives the objective, without breathing a soul of sentiment through it, are both on the lowest step from which poetry goes down into the prose of common life.

Criticism.

I am more and more convinced that, whenever one has to vent an opinion on the actions or on the writings of others, unless this be done from a certain one-sided enthusiasm, or from a loving interest in the person and the work, the result is hardly worth gathering up. Sympathy and enjoyment in what we see is in fact the only reality, and from such reality, reality as a natural product follows. All else is vanity.

Lyrical Poetry.

All good lyrics must be reasonable as a whole, and yet in details a little unreasonable.

The Moral and the Beautiful—Sophocles.

How came the moral element into the world? Through God Himself, like everything else. It is no product of human reflection, but a beauty of nature inherent and inborn. It is, more or less, the dower of mankind generally, but existed to a high degree in a few eminently gifted minds. These have, by great deeds or doctrines, manifested its divine nature; which, then, by the beauty of its appearance, won the love of men, and powerfully attracted them to reverence and emulation.

Alongside of this contagion from superior natures, a consciousness of the worth of the morally beautiful and good could be attained by experience, inasmuch as the bad showed itself in its consequences as a destroyer of happiness, both in individuals and the whole body, while the noble and right seemed to produce and secure the happiness of one and all. Thus the morally beautiful could become a doctrine, and diffuse itself over whole nations as a sort of code formally enunciated.

It has been stated by some writers that the Greek tragedy made moral beauty a special object; but it was not so much morality as pure humanity in its whole extent, especially in positions where, by falling into contact with rude power, it could assume a tragic character. In this region, indeed, the moral element stood as the principal factor of human nature.

The morality of Antigone, besides, was not invented by Sophocles, but was contained in the subject, which Sophocles chose the more readily, as it united so much dramatic effect with moral beauty.

Poetry and History.

MANZONI wants nothing except to know what a good poet he is, and what rights belong to him as such. He has too much respect for history, and on this account is always adding notes to his pieces, in which he shows how faithful he has been to detail. Now, though his facts may be historical, his characters are not so, any more than my Thoas and Iphigenia. No poet has ever known the historical characters which he has painted; if he had, he could scarcely have made use of them. The poet must know what effects he wishes to produce, and regulate the nature of his characters accordingly. If I had tried to make Egmont as history represents him, the father of a dozen children, his light-minded proceedings would have appeared very absurd. I needed an Egmont more in harmony with his own actions and my poetic views; and this is, as Clara says, *my* Egmont.

What would be the use of poets, if they only repeated the record of the historian? The poet must go further, and give us, if possible, something higher and better. All the characters of SOPHOCLES bear something of that poet's lofty soul; and it is the same with the characters of SHAKESPEARE. This is as it ought to be. Nay, Shakespeare goes further, and makes his Romans Englishmen; and there too he is right, for otherwise his nation would not have understood him.

Poetry.

What makes poetry? A full heart, brimful of one noble passion.

Scott.

You find everywhere in Scott a remarkable security and thoroughness in his delineation, which proceeds from his comprehensive knowledge of the real world, obtained by life-long studies and observations, and a daily discussion of the most important relations. Then come his great talent and his comprehensive nature. You remember the English critic, who compares the poets to the voices of male singers, of which some can command only a few fine tones, while others have the whole compass, from the highest to the lowest, completely in their power. Scott is one of this last sort. In the 'Fair Maid of Perth,' you will not find a single weak passage to make you feel as if his knowledge and talent were insufficient. He is equal to his subject in every direction in which it takes him; the king, the royal brother, the prince, the head of the clergy, the nobles, the magistracy, the citizens and mechanics, the Highlanders, are all drawn with the same sure hand, and hit off with equal truth.

The Idea in Poetry—Faust.

My countrymen, who have a peculiar rage for the idea in all things, are continually asking me what idea I meant to embody in my Faust? as if I knew myself, and could inform them. *From heaven, through the world, to hell,* would indeed be something; but this is no idea, only a course of action. And further, that the devil loses the wager, and that a man, continually struggling from degrading error towards something better, should be redeemed, is an effective, and to many a good and elevating thought; but it is no idea which lies at the foundation of the whole, and of every individual scene. It would have been a fine thing indeed if I had strung so rich, varied, and highly diversified a life as I have brought to view in Faust upon the slender string of one pervading idea!

It was, in short, not in my line as a poet to strive to embody anything abstract. I received into my soul certain impressions, vivid, varied, and pleasant, just as a lively imagination presented them; and I had as a poet nothing more to do than artistically to round off and elaborate such views and impressions, and by means of a lively representation so to bring them forward that others might be impressed in a like way.

Byron.

With that disposition which always leads him into the illimitable, the restraint which he imposed upon himself by the observance of the three unities becomes him very well. If he had but known how to endure moral restraints also! That he could not do this was his ruin; and it may be aptly said, that he was destroyed by his own unbridled temperament.

But he was too much in the dark about himself. He lived impetuously for the day, and neither knew nor thought what he was doing. Permitting everything to himself, and excusing nothing in others, he necessarily put himself in a bad position, and made the world his foe. At the very beginning, he offended the most distinguished literary men by his "English Bards and Scotch Reviewers." To be permitted only to live after this, he was obliged to go back a step. In his succeeding works he continued in the path of opposition and fault-finding. Church and State were not left unassailed. This reckless conduct drove him from England, and would in time have driven him from Europe also. Everywhere things were too narrow for him, and with the most perfect personal freedom he felt himself confined; this world seemed to him a prison. His Grecian expedition was the result of no voluntary resolution; his misunderstanding with the world drove him to it.

The renunciation of what was hereditary and patriotic not only caused the personal destruction of so distinguished a man, but his revolutionary turn, and the constant mental agitation with which it was combined, did not allow his talent a fair development. Moreover, his perpetual negation and fault-finding is injurious even to his excellent works. For not only does the discontent of the poet infect the reader, but the end of all opposition is negation; and negation is nothing. If I call *bad* bad, what do I gain? but if I call *good* bad, I do a great deal of mischief. He who will work aright must never rail, must not trouble himself at all about what is ill done, but only do well himself; for the great point is not to pull down, but to build up, and in this humanity finds pure joy. Lord Byron is to be regarded as a man, as an Englishman, as a peer, and as a great talent. His good qualities belong chiefly to the man; his bad to the Englishman and the peer; his talent is incommensurable.

All Englishmen are, as such, without reflection, properly so called. Distractions of various kinds and party spirit will not allow their thoughts to ripen in quiet. But they are great as practical men.

Thus Lord Byron could never attain to wise reflection on himself or on the world. But where he creates he always succeeds; and we may truly say that with him inspiration supplies the place of reflection. He was always obliged to go on poetising; and then everything that came from him, especially from his heart, was excellent. He produced his best things, as women do pretty children, without thinking about it or knowing how it was done.

He is a great talent, a born talent; and I never saw the true poetical power greater in any man than in him. In the apprehension of external objects, and a clear penetration into past situations, he is quite as great as Shakespeare. But as a pure individual, Shakespeare is his superior. This was felt by Byron, and on this account he does not say much of Shakespeare, although he knows whole passages by heart. He would willingly have denied him altogether; for Shakespeare's cheerfulness is in his way, and he feels that he is no match for it. Pope he does not deny, for he had no cause to fear him. On the contrary, he mentions him, and shows him respect when he can; for he knows well enough that Pope is a mere foil to himself. His high rank as an English peer was very injurious to Byron; for every talent is oppressed by the outer world; how much more, then, when there is such high birth and so great a fortune? A certain middle rank is much more favourable to talent, on which account we find all great artists and poets in the middle classes. Byron's predilection for the unbounded could not have been nearly so dangerous with more humble birth and smaller means. But as it was, he was able to put every fancy into practice, and this involved him in innumerable scrapes. Besides, how could one of such high rank be inspired with awe and respect by any rank whatever? He spoke out whatever he felt, and this brought him into ceaseless conflict with the world.

If Lord Byron had had an opportunity of working off all the opposition in his character by a number of strong parliamentary speeches, he would have been much more pure as a poet. But as he hardly ever spoke in Parliament, he kept within himself all his feelings against his patrons; and to free himself from them, he had no other means than to express them in poetical form. I could therefore call a great part of Byron's poetry works of negation, speeches that should have been delivered in Parliament; and to place them under this rubric would rather add to than take from their reputation.

The Poet's Function—Elective Affinities.

The very simple text, of which my novel, 'The Elective Affinities,' is a paraphrase, reads thus: (Matt. v. 28)—*Whosoever looks on a woman to lust after her has committed adultery with her already in his heart.* Whether any one, among its numerous readers and critics, has ever recognised this text behind the paraphrase I cannot tell. The public never can be made to understand that the true poet is only a masked father confessor, whose special function is to exhibit what is dangerous in sentiment and pernicious in action, by a vivid picture of their consequences. Before the moral significance of a true work of art can be generally apprehended, a much higher degree of culture on the part of the public must be attained. To understand this sort of confession, in fact, the reader must have been trained to play the part of father confessor to himself.

Advice to Young Poets.

Have a care of devoting yourself to a *great work*. The itch of producing an *opus magnum* has ruined, and ruins, many of our finest poetical talents. I have suffered somewhat from this disease myself. How many gems of thought have fallen into the well while I was vainly planning some fancied *monumentum ære perennius!* Had I written all that the favourable spirit moved me to write, no hundred volumes would have been space for it.

The present moment will have its rights; the thoughts and feelings that daily crowd round the mind of a true poet are entitled to an expression as free as is their visiting. But, with a great work in gestation, nothing else can be attended to; all thoughts, however good, are rejected, that do not bear upon that one object; the comfortable enjoyment of life is for a time suspended. How much intellectual strength must we not put forth, merely to lay out and round off the plan of a great whole; and when this is done, how seldom do we find the favourable moment in which power of thought unites with quiet of mind to produce a full, unbroken stream of poetic expression! Very often the poet finds, after years of thought and labour, that he has mistaken himself in his whole subject, and then his work is altogether useless; or perhaps, though successful in some parts, where the materials are so extensive, he fails in others; and in this case his work wants completeness as a whole, and the good suffers owing to its conjunction with the bad. The labour and sacrifice of half a lifetime may thus produce nothing but discomfort and mortification. If, on the other hand, the poet takes hold of the present as it offers itself, he cannot fail to breathe through his handiwork some of the freshness of reality, and snatch some fugitive trait of nature; or should he be so unfortunate as to please neither himself nor his friends, why, then, he may throw the blotted paper into the fire to-day, and write upon parchment to-morrow.

Be faithful in little, but let that little be fresh and true, and no day will pass without its balsam of poetic enjoyment. Do not consider yourself too high even for the Annuals or the Magazines, but always follow your own plan, and write *to*, not *for*, the public.

The world is so great and so rich, and life is so manifold, that there will be no want of suitable occasions for poems. But your little pieces must be in the true sense of the word *Gelegenheits-gedichte*,— they must arise from, and have reference to, an actual occasion of life,—reality must afford both the origination of their existence and the materials out of which they are moulded. A special case requires nothing but the treatment of a poet to become universal and poetical. *All my poems are Gelegenheits-gedichte; they were all motived by, and have all their root and base in, reality.* Of poems that are conjured out of the air I make no account.

Let me not be told that the actual world is destitute of a poetic interest. It is the great triumph of genius to make the common appear novel by opening our eyes to its beauty. Reality gives the motive, the hinging points, the kernel; but to create a beautiful living whole out of these rough materials, that is the work of the poet.

Kotzebue.

What has lasted for twenty years, and still preserves its popularity, cannot be destitute of something substantially good. When he remained in his own proper sphere, and did not venture beyond his depth, Kotzebue always produced something good. He and Chodowiecki were of kindred genius; both were masters in painting characters and scenes of everyday life; but when they meddled with the Greeks and the Romans, they made themselves and their heroes ridiculous. You have mentioned his *Verwandschaften* and his *Versöhnung;* the *Klingsberge* is my favourite piece. Whatever may be said against

Kotzebue, one thing cannot be denied—he walked through life with his eyes open.

Poetry as Individualism.

The really high and difficult part of art is the apprehension of what is individual—characteristic. The young poet must do some sort of violence to himself to get out of the mere general idea. No doubt this is difficult; but it is the very life of art. Besides, when you content yourself with generalities, any one can imitate you; but in the particular, no one can. And why? Because no others have experienced exactly the same thing. And you need not fear lest what is peculiar should not meet with sympathy. Each character, however peculiar it may be, and each object which you can represent from the stone up to man, has generality; for there is repetition everywhere, and there is nothing to be found only once in the world.

Poetry and Philosophy—Schiller.

I have a peculiar feeling towards Schiller. Some scenes of his great drama I read with peculiar love and admiration; but presently I meet with something which violates the truth of nature, and I can go no further. I feel this even in reading "Wallenstein." I cannot but think that Schiller's turn for philosophy injured his poetry, because it led him to consider speculation far higher than all nature—indeed thus to annihilate nature. What he could conceive must happen, whether in conformity with nature or not.

The Theatre.

The *theatre* has often been at variance with the *pulpit;* they ought not, I think, to quarrel. How much is it to be wished that in both, the celebration of NATURE and of GOD were intrusted to none but men of noble minds!

The Theatre and the State.

How useful might the theatre be made to all ranks! What advantage even the State might procure from it, if the occupations, trades, and undertakings of men were brought upon the stage, and presented on their praiseworthy side, in that point of view from which the State itself would honour and protect them! As matters stand, we exhibit only the ridiculous side of men. The comic poet is but a spiteful tax-gatherer, who keeps a watchful eye over the errors of his fellow-subjects, and seems gratified when he can fix any charge upon them. Might it not be a worthy and pleasing task for a statesman to survey the natural and reciprocal influences of all classes on each other, and to find some poet gifted with sufficient humour, to represent these worthily?

In this way, I am persuaded, many very entertaining, both agreeable and useful pieces, might be executed. But so far as I, in wandering about the world, have been able to observe, statesmen are accustomed merely to forbid, to hinder, to refuse; but very rarely to invite, to further, to reward. They let all things go along, till some mischief happen; then they get into a fume, and lay about them.

Theatrical Enjoyment.

Any one who is sufficiently young, and who is not quite spoiled, could not easily find any place that would suit him so well as a theatre. No one asks you any questions; you need not open your mouth unless you choose; on the contrary, you sit quite at your ease like a king, letting everything pass before you, and recreating your mind and senses to your heart's content. There is poetry, there is painting, there are singing and music, there is acting,—and what not besides. When all these arts, and the charm of youth and beauty heightened to an important degree, work in concert on the same evening, it is a bouquet with which no other can compare. But even when part is bad and part is good, it is still better than looking out of a window, or playing a game at whist in a close room amid the smoke of cigars.

Actors.

I pardon in the player every fault that springs from self-deception and the wish to please. If he seems not something to himself and others, he is nothing. To seem is his vocation; he must prize his momentary approbation highly, for he gets no other recompense. He must try to glitter; he is there to do so.

Criticism—Shakespeare.

Many of the wonders of Shakespeare's genius are due to the powerfully productive atmosphere of his age and time. It is with Shakespeare as with the mountains of Switzerland. Transplant Mont Blanc at once into the large plain of the Luneburg Heath, and we should find no words to express our wonder at its magnitude. Seek it, however, in its gigantic home—go to it over its immense neighbours, the Jungfrau, the Finsteraarhorn, the Eiger, the Wetterhorn, St Gothard, and Monte Rosa; Mont Blanc will, indeed, still remain a giant, but it will no longer produce such amazement in the spectator.

Besides, let him who will not believe that much of Shakespeare's greatness appertains to his age, only ask himself the question, whether a phenomenon so astounding would be possible in the present England of 1824, in these evil days of criticising and hair-splitting journals.

That undisturbed, innocent, somnambulatory production, by which alone anything great can thrive, is no longer possible. Our talents at present lie before the public. The daily criticisms which appear in fifty different places, and the gossip that is caused by them amongst the public, prevent the appearance of any sound production. In the present day, he who does not keep aloof from all this, and isolate himself by main force, is lost. Through the bad, chiefly negative, æsthetical and critical tone of the journals, a sort of half culture finds its way into the masses; but to productive talent it is a noxious mist, a dropping poison, which destroys the tree of creative power, from the ornamental green leaves to the deepest pith and the most hidden fibres.

And then how tame and weak has life itself become during the last two shabby centuries! Where do we now meet an original character, and where is the man who has the strength to be true, and to show himself as he is? This specially affects the poet, leading him to quarry his own mind resolutely, in order to find some compensation for the featureless tameness of the outer world.

Originality.

People are always talking about originality; but what do they mean? As soon as we are born, the world begins to work upon us, and this goes on to the end. And after all, what can we call our own except energy, strength, and will? If I could give an account of all that I owe to great predecessors and contemporaries, there would be but a small balance in my favour.

However, the time of life in which we are subjected to a new and important personal influence is by no means a matter of indifference. That Lessing, Winckelmann, and Kant were older than I, and that the first two acted upon my youth, the latter on my advanced age,—this circumstance was for me very important. Again, that Schiller was so much younger than I, and engaged in his freshest strivings just as I began to be weary of the world,—just, too, as the brothers Von Humboldt and Schlegel were beginning their career under my eye,—was of the greatest importance; and I derived from it unspeakable advantages.

Carlyle.

It is admirable in Carlyle, that in his judgment of our German authors he has especially in view the *mental and moral core*, as that which is really influential. Carlyle is a moral force of great importance. There is in him much for the future; and we cannot foresee what he will produce and effect.

Criticism.

No person can form a judgment of history who has not lived through history. So it is with whole nations.

The Germans learned first to form a judgment on literary matters, when they had a literature of their own.

Literature—Over-production.

I cannot but look upon it as one of the greatest misfortunes of our age, that it allows nothing to ripen quietly; that the next moment, so to speak, devours the preceding; that no time is allowed for digestion; and that we live from hand to mouth, without leisure to bring forth any finished product. Have we not reviews and magazines for every hour of the day? By this portentous machinery, everything that a man does or writes, or intends to do or write, is forthwith dragged before the public. No man dare do anything, enjoy or suffer anything, save for the delectation of others; and thus every trifle goes from house to house, from town to town, from kingdom to kingdom, from one quarter of the world to another, at a galloping speed.

As in the mechanical world one cannot stop the progress of steam and machinery, so also in the domain of morals: the liveliness of commerce, the facilities of paper money, the making of debts to pay debts, these are the overwhelming forces with which a young man in the present day has to contend. Well for him if nature has gifted him with a moderate, cool, quiet temper, so that he may neither make immoderate demands on the world nor suffer himself to be moved by it.

Public Speaking.

To Rhetoric are given all the faculties of poetry and all its privileges; she seizes on them and abuses them, that she may gain certain superficial moral or perhaps immoral advantages in political life.

Popular Songs and Ballads.

The special value of what we call *National Songs* or *Ballads* is, that their inspiration comes fresh from nature. They are never got up; they flow from a sure spring. The poet of a literary age might avail himself of this advantage if he only knew how. There is always one thing, however, in which the former assert their advantage. The unsophisticated man is more the master of direct effective expression in few words than he who has received a regular literary training.

Literature—Style.

On the whole, philosophical speculation is injurious to the Germans, as it tends to make their style vague, difficult, and obscure. The stronger their attachment to certain philosophical schools, the worse they write. Those Germans who, as men of business and actual life, confine themselves to the practical, write the best. Schiller's style is most noble and impressive when he leaves off philosophising, as I observe every day in his highly interesting letters, with which I am now busy.

There are likewise among the German women genial creatures who write a really excellent style, and, indeed, in that respect surpass many of our celebrated male writers. The English almost always write well—being born orators and practical men, with a tendency to the real.

The French, in their style, remain true to their general character. They are of a social nature, and therefore never forget the public whom they address: they strive to be clear, that they may convince their reader,—agreeable, that they may please him.

Altogether, the style of a writer is a faithful representative of his mind; therefore, if any man wishes to write a clear style, let him first be clear in his thoughts; and, if any would write in a noble style, let him first possess a noble soul, and live a noble life.

Prose.

Very few of our recent young poets write good *prose*. This is very easily explained. To write prose one must have something to say; but he who has nothing to say can still twirl verses and find rhymes, where one word suggests the other, and at last something comes out, which in fact is nothing, but which looks as if it were something.

Prose and Poetry.

If imagination did not originate things which must ever remain problems to the understanding, there would be but little for the imagination to do. It is this which separates *poetry* from *prose;* in which latter understanding always is, and always should be, dominant.

Language—Style.

It is not language in itself and independently which is accurate, vigorous, lucid, or graceful, but the spirit which is embodied in it; and so it is not in every one's power to give to his opinions, speeches, or poems, the good qualities of expression that ought to belong to them. The question is, whether nature has given the writer or speaker intellectual and moral qualities that demand and shape out for themselves such an embodiment — intellectual powers of intuition and penetration; and not less moral power, that he may be able to resist the evil demons who would hinder him in the unswerving loyalty that he must pay to truth.

Literature.

Literature is the fragment of fragments. The smallest part of what has been done and spoken has been recorded; and the smallest part of what has been recorded has survived.

Genius.

No productiveness of the highest kind, no remarkable discovery, no great thought which bears fruit and has results, is in the power of any one: such things are elevated above all earthly control. Man must consider them as an unexpected gift from above, as the pure efflux of divine grace which he must receive and venerate with joyful thanks. They are akin to the δαίμων, or genius of life, which does with him what it pleases, and to which he unconsciously resigns himself, whilst he believes he is acting from his own impulse. In such cases, man may best be considered as an instrument in the higher government of the world, as a vessel found worthy for the reception of a divine influence. I say this while I consider how often a single thought has given a different form to whole centuries; and how individual men have, by their expressions, imprinted a stamp upon their age, which has remained uneffaced, and has operated beneficially upon many succeeding generations.

Shakespeare.

Goethe showed me a very interesting English work, which illustrated all Shakespeare in copperplates. Each page embraced, in six small designs, one piece with small verses written beneath, so that the leading idea and the most important situations of each work were brought before the eyes. All these immortal tragedies and comedies thus passed before us like processions in a masque.

It is overpowering, he said, to look through these little pictures. Thus for the first time we are made to feel the infinite wealth and grandeur of this man's mind. There is no motive in human life which he has not exhibited and expressed. And all with what ease and freedom!

But we cannot talk about Shakespeare; all speech is inadequate. I have touched upon the subject in my 'Wilhelm Meister'; but that is not saying much. He is not a theatrical poet; he never thought of the stage; it was far too narrow for his great mind—nay, the whole visible world was too narrow.

He is even too rich and too powerful. A productive nature ought not to read more than one of his dramas in a year, if it would not be wrecked entirely. I did well to get rid of him by writing Goetz and Egmont; and Byron did well by not having too much respect and admiration for him, but going his own way. How many excellent Germans have been ruined by him and Calderon!

Shakespeare gives us golden apples in silver salvers. We get, indeed, the silver salvers by studying his works; but, unfortunately, we have only potatoes to put into them.

Talent and the World.

The world cannot get on without men of talent; and yet they don't treat them very well when they have them.

Subjective Poets.

Why poets are like bears? because
They're always sucking their own claws.

Poetry and Melancholy.

The bright sunbeam, in shower of tears,
On a dark ground of cloud appears;
And this explains, if you would know it,
The moody cast that marks the poet.

Sickly Poets.

Bah! I can't stand such sickly trash:
  Your books no doubt in tropes are wealthy;
But ere you write again, my son,
  Learn to be happy first and healthy.

Popularity.

Build for the future, and you may
Earn scanty plaudits from to-day;
But serve the present, and you will
Pile pence and praise to glorify your skill.

A bitter Critic.

Whose blame is bitter, and whose praise is scanty?
The man who tried and failed—a *dilettante!*

Poets.

What gives the poet power to move all hearts,
Each stubborn element to sway,
What but the harmony, his being's inmost tone,
That charms all feelings back into his own?
Where listless Nature, her eternal thread,
The unwilling spindle twists around,
And hostile shocks of things that will not wed
With jarring dissonance resound,
Who guides with living pulse the rhythmic flow
Of powers that make sweet music as they go?
Who consecrates each separate limb and soul
To beat in glorious concert with the whole?
Who makes the surgy-swelling billow
Heave with the wildly heaving breast,
And on the evening's rosy pillow,
Invites the brooding heart to rest?
Who scatters spring's most lovely blooms upon
The path of the belovèd one?
Who plaits the leaves that unregarded grow
Into a crown to deck the honoured brow?
Who charms the gods? who makes Olympus yield?
The power of man in poet's art revealed.

Poetry and Youth.

Then give me back the years again,
When mine own spirit too was growing,
When my whole being was a vein
Of native songs within me flowing!
Then slept the world in misty blue,
Each bud the nascent wonder cherished,
And all for me the flowerets grew,
That on each meadow richly flourished.
Though I had nothing then, I had a treasure,
The thirst for truth, and in illusion pleasure.
Give me the free, unshackled pinion,
The height of joy, the depth of pain,
Strong hate, and stronger love's dominion;
Oh give me back my youth again!

Limitation.

Not for untutored souls that scorn restraint
The bays that bind high-honoured brows may grow;
But who would pluck the topmost Praise must learn
To lord his passion, and to rein his bent,
Have all his powers in hand, and bow with awe
To the free spirit's free self-sanctioned Law.

Literature and Faction.

Lutheran rage is lulled; but now French fever is rampant;
Sacred or secular strifes murder the Muses the same.

Genus Irritabile Vatum.

I know him well; not hard is he to know,
Too proud to mask himself. You see him sink
Into himself, as if he held the world
In his sole bosom, in himself complete
A compact world, and all around him else
Vanished in blank indifference. It may rise
Or fall or float at large, no whit cares he—
When lo! all in a minute, as when a mine
Fires at a spark, at touch of joy or sorrow,
Anger or whim, he breaks into a flame:
And then what he would grasp must own his hold,
And all things be that he thinks ought to be,
And in a moment to his wish must rise
What for long years in the slow womb of time
Needs silent preparation. From himself,
He with ingenious wilfulness demands
The impossible, that he may have a right
To ask the same from others. He would bind
The two ends of all things with hasty bond
In his soul, a task which in a million men
One may achieve—and *he* is not the man;
But, clutching madly at the stars, he falls
Back to the earth, no bigger than before.

Originality.

You're a disciple of no school,
And own no living master's rule;

Nor have dead men in Greece or Rome
Taught you things better learned at home;
This means, if I am not mistaking—
You're a prime fool of your own making.

Critics.

Did I, when you went a-warring,
   Bid your bloody battles cease?
Did I make loud protestation,
   When your Congress patched a peace?

Did I tell the practised angler
   Where to fling his baited line?
Did I give the wright instructions
   Where to split, and where to join?

But *you* will give me directions
   How to read and how to write
From the mighty book which Nature
   Opened to the poet's sight.

If you have the poet's vision,
   Show what thing God showed to you;
But, if my work you would measure,
   First learn what I meant to do.

Poetry.

Poetry is a gushing well
   That scorns the niggard measure,
Keeps the blood warm, and makes it swell
   In pulsing veins of pleasure.

Blame me not!—the cup of sorrow,
   When it comes to me,
I can sip, nor need to borrow
   Modest airs from thee.

Modesty's a pretty thing
   In a maid when wooed;
Modestly she folds her wing
   From handling coarse and rude.

And sober thought, the wise man says,
   In wise hour teaches me
For time to order well my days,
   And for eternity.

But rhyme disowns the sober mood;
   I love to rhyme alone,
Or with one friend or two whose blood
   Flows kindly with my own!

Cowled or uncowled, let preachers come
    To dam my foaming river;
They may prevail to make me dumb,
    But to be sober never!

When the poet's fancy burns,
    Be slow to reprimand him;
You'll forgive his wildest turns,
    When once you understand him!

PHILOSOPHY, METAPHYSICS, LOGIC, TRUTH, AND SCIENCE

Alle Philosophie muss gelebt und geliebt werden.

PHILOSOPHY, METAPHYSICS, LOGIC, TRUTH, AND SCIENCE.

Spiritualism—Moral Magnetism.

WE all walk in mysteries. We are surrounded by an atmosphere of which we do not know what is stirring in it, or how it is connected with our own spirit. So much is certain—that in particular cases we can put out the feelers of our soul beyond its bodily limits, and that a presentiment—nay, an actual insight—into the immediate future is accorded to it.

Besides, one soul may have a decided influence upon another merely by means of its silent presence, of which I could relate many instances. It has often happened to me that, when I have been walking with an acquaintance, and have had a living image of something in my mind, he has at once begun to speak of that very thing. I have also known a man who, without saying a word, could suddenly silence a party engaged in cheerful conversation by the mere power of his mind. Nay, he could also introduce a tone which would make everybody feel uncomfortable. We have all something of electric and magnetic forces within us, and we put forth, like the magnet itself, an attractive or repulsive power accordingly, as we come in contact with something similar or dissimilar. It is possible, nay, even probable, that if a young girl were, without knowing it, to find herself in a dark chamber with a man who designed to murder her, she would have an uneasy sense of his unknown presence, and that an anguish would come over her which would drive her from the room to the family parlour.

Metaphysics.

Man must always in some sense cling to the belief that the unknowable is knowable, otherwise speculation would cease.

The universal and the particular are one. The particular is the universal, seen under special conditions.

Truth.

It is not always necessary that truth should be embodied; enough if it hover, spirit-like, around us and produce harmony; if it float through the air like the sweetly solemn chiming of a minster bell.

To understand that the sky is everywhere blue, we need not go round the world.

One need not see or live through everything for himself; only, if we chose to confide in others, and in their representations, we must remember that we have in such case to do with three things — the matter on hand and two persons.

There are not a few persons in the world who, if they had not felt themselves bound to repeat what is untrue, simply because they had once said it, would have become something quite different from what they are.

What is not true has this advantage, that it can be eternally talked about; whereas about truth there is an urgency that cries out for its application; for otherwise it has no right to be there.

Aristotle and the Greeks.

When we look at the problems of ARISTOTLE, we are amazed by the powers of observation of the Greeks, and how they had eyes for everything. They were possessed, however, by the vice of hasty generalisation, leaping from the phenomenon direct to the conclusion; and in this way many inadequate theories were allowed to assert themselves. This is a vice, however, to which human nature even at the present day is scarcely less prone.

The Germans.

The Germans have, above all other nations, the art of making the sciences inaccessible to the people.

Causes and Effects.

Man finds himself in the midst of a multitude of effects, and cannot refrain from searching out their causes. As an easy-going creature, he grasps at what is nearest to him, and rests satisfied with that. This procedure is that known in philosophical books as the common-sense method.

Teleology—Design—Final Causes.

It is natural to man to look upon himself as the chief end of the creation, and to look upon all other things as existing only in reference to the service and the utility which they may be of to him. He appropriates the vegetable and the animal world; and while he devours other creatures as suitable nourishment to himself, he acknowledges God, and praises the goodness which in such a fatherly style has provided for mankind. From the cow he takes milk, from the bee honey, from the sheep wool; and while he gets from the creature a result useful to himself, readily assumes that it was created solely for that purpose. Nay, he can scarcely imagine that even the smallest weed that grows has not some relation to himself; and though he may not be able at present to see how its existence serves his need, he believes that one day its special character of subserviency to human wants will be made apparent.

And as man thinks in general, so also in special domains of inquiry, he without hesitation transfers his principle of judging in the affairs of common life into the field of science; and accordingly, sets himself to search after the special aim and utility of each individual member or part of every organic being.

This will pass very well for a time, and even perform good service to science; but by-and-by he will stumble upon phenomena, where such a narrow and partial view proves inadequate, and where, without any higher clue, he will find himself entangled in sheer contradictions. Such utilitarian doctors say, No doubt the ox has horns to butt with them; and then, I ask, Why has the sheep none? and when it happens to have any, Why are they twisted round the ear so as to be of no use?

It is an altogether different matter, however, when I say the ox butts with its horns because it has them.

To ask the object for which anything exists, to put the question WHY, is altogether unscientific.

With the question HOW, on the other hand, we

advance further; for, when I ask how the ox has horns, this leads me to the consideration of his organisation, and teaches me at the same time why the lion has no horns, and cannot possibly have them.

In the same way man has in his skull two cavities which are not filled up. In this case the question WHY, for what purpose, would be of little avail. But the question How teaches me that these cavities are remains of the animal skull, which in the lower organisations are found in greater quantity, and of which even in the high development which man presents, vestiges remain.

The utilitarian doctors would think they had lost their God if they were not to worship that Being who gave the ox horns to butt with; but let them allow me to worship Him who in the wealth of His creativeness was so great, that after thousands of plants had grown, He could produce one which contained the excellences of all the rest, and who, after creating thousands of animals, could crown the array with one that contained them all—namely, Man.

Let these persons worship that great Being who gives grass to the cow, and food and drink to man, as much as he can enjoy. I worship Him rather who has put such a power of productiveness into the world that, if only the millionth part of it assumes reality, the world still swarms with creatures to such an extent, that neither war, nor pestilence, nor inundation, nor conflagration, can have any sensible effect in destroying it. That is my God.[1]

Truth—Knowledge.

LESSING, who felt painfully many cramping limitations in life, makes one of his characters say, *no man must* MUST. To this a man of an alert and active mind replied, *who wills must.* A third, certainly a man of culture, added, whoever *understands clearly wills also;* and in this way they thought to have completed the entire circle of KNOWLEDGE, WILL, and NECESSITY. But in general a man's knowledge fixes his course of action; and therefore nothing is more terrible than to see ignorance in action.

Authority.

Authority—viz., the fact that a thing has already been done, said, or decided—has a high value; but only a formalist asks for authority to help him to a decision in all possible cases.

---

[1] The difference between a true and an artificial teleology is well expressed by a recent writer: "We understand the egg by thinking of the chicken, but this is not to explain eggs by omelettes." Ritchie, in 'Essays on Philosophical Criticism:' London, 1833. In other words—divine ends are one thing, human appropriation another.—J. S. B.

Opinions.

Since nothing is so important to people as their opinions, every one who propounds an opinion looks about him right and left for props with which to support it. Of TRUTH he makes use, as long as he finds it serviceable; but seizes upon *falsehood* with a passionate *rhetoric*, if only it can be used with a look of *logic* to fling a glamour in the eyes of the contradictor, or even to serve as a convenient stop-gap for the nonce.

Reason and Judgment.

The *reason* has to do with things in the process of *evolution;* judgment with things evolved. The one does not vex itself with the question, *for what purpose?* the other does not ask, *from what source?* The one rejoices in the discovery of a cause, the other in the application of a result.

Analogy.

Analogy has two errors to fear,—the one when it contents itself with being serviceable to wit, in which case it floats away in futile sport; the other, when it shrouds itself in tropes and similes: this last is the less dangerous of the two.

Myths.

Neither *myths* nor legends are to be tolerated in *science;* let us then leave to the poet, whose province it is, to use them for the benefit and amusement of the world. The scientific man should limit himself to the nearest and clearest material that lies before him. If, however, he chooses occasionally to come forth in the oratorical vein, this also may be allowed him, provided he remembers what he is about.

Truth—Science.

Much confusion in science, and in everything else, arises from this, that men who have no capacity for thought will presume to theorise, because they cannot see that mere stores of *knowledge*, however vast, in themselves give no capacity for *thinking*. Such persons, at starting, will go on working with a fair amount of common-sense, and succeed pretty well; but common-sense has its limits, beyond which, when it passes, it is in danger of becoming absurd. The province of common-sense is active life. In action it will not lightly go wrong; but the higher regions of thought, speculation, and large conclusions, are altogether outside of its jurisdiction.

A historical feeling for humanity is that in which a large natural sympathy has been so cultivated, that in its judgments of contemporary worth the merits of the past are fairly brought into consideration. One must bear in mind that there are many persons who will insist on saying something original, without possessing any genuine productive faculty; hence the strangest attempts at cleverness, and striking feats of real cleverness without truth, or motive, or love, are constantly thrusting themselves into view.

Earnest and profoundly thoughtful men can never expect to find it easy to gain for themselves a favourable position as against the general public.

Every great idea, as soon as it realises itself, works tyrannically; hence the benefits with which it was fraught are only too soon changed into evils. Bearing this in mind, any man may find it easy to defend or extol any institution, if he only recalls its beginnings, and gives himself some pains to demonstrate that all the excellence which gave a charm to its birth remains unchanged in its continued existence.

Physics and Metaphysics.

There are not a few problems in the *natural sciences* of which a man cannot speak justly without calling metaphysics to his aid; not technical words about knowing and being, such as make a show in the schools, but that wisdom of thought which was before all physics, lives with it, and will endure after it.

Natural and Artificial Vision.

Microscopes and *telescopes*, properly considered, put our human eyes out of their natural, healthy, and profitable point of view.

Silence.

I look on and hold my tongue about many things, because I would not disturb others in their faith or enjoyment, and am content that they should find pleasure in what is distasteful to me.

Philology.

The business of the philologer is to exercise his wit on the congruity of written tradition. The written document lies at the foundation; and with it even gaps and slips of the pen, which obscure the sense of the passage—everything, in short, that may be defective in a manuscript. A second copy is found, and a third; and the comparison of these makes ever more apparent the meaning and significance of the matter handed down. The scholar goes yet farther, and demands of his inner judgment that, apart from external aid, it shall make more and more clear the significance of the matter submitted to interpretation. For this a certain tact and insight into ancient authors are necessary; also a certain degree of inventiveness; so that one must not blame him, if he sometimes claims for himself the right to decide on points purely æsthetical — in which domain, however, he must not expect always to succeed.[1]

Experience.

He who will be content with actual experience has light enough. The growing child is in this sense wise.

Theory.

Theory is of no use in itself; but only in so far as it helps us to believe in the coherency of phenomena.

Philosophy—Plato and Aristotle.

Plato is not so much a citizen of this world, as a blessed spirit, whom it has pleased for a certain period to make his lodgment here. It is not so much his business to know the world, which he rather presupposes, as to communicate to us, in a kindly way, those fundamental typical truths which he has brought with him from a higher sphere. He plunges into the deep places of our existence here, more with

---

[1] German scholarship abounds with examples of ingenious impertinence, caused by the confounding of these two essentially diverse functions.—J. S. B.

the view of filling its voids with his fulness, than to make investigations and inductions. His tendency is always upward, possessed constantly with a longing to return to his divine home. Every word that he utters has reference to a totality of the good, the beautiful, and the true, the growth of which in every human breast it is his grand object to promote. What he appropriates to himself of merely earthly knowledge, melts, or one might even say exhales, in his method and in his style.

Aristotle, on the other hand, stands to the world in the relation of a man like ourselves—an architect. He finds himself here, once for all, with the destiny to work and to organise. As an architect he examines the soil carefully, but not farther than is required for his foundation. What may be found deeper down to the centre of the earth is no concern of his. For his architecture he encloses a tremendous breadth of ground, brings in materials from all quarters, arranges them skilfully, and piles them up with the solid masonry of a pyramid; while Plato shoots into the upper regions, like an obelisk or a spire of flame.

When such a pair of men, who in a fashion divided humanity among themselves, as separate representatives of admirable qualities of intellect, not easily united in one character, had the good fortune to grow up into a perfect culture, and to put forth the abundant fruit of that culture, not merely in short laconic aphorisms and maxims, but in various works largely conceived, and executed with extraordinary comprehensiveness and completeness; and when these works were not lost, but remained extant for the benefit of mankind, so as to be made the constant subject of study and contemplation;—under such circumstances it necessarily follows that the world in its thinking and feeling capacity was necessitated to attach itself to the one or the other of these two representative men, acknowledging him as master, teacher, and guide.

This necessity, under which the human mind lay, of submitting itself to be moulded by these two Titanic intellects, appears most strikingly in the history of Bible hermeneutics. The sacred volume, with the wonderful independence, entire originality, many-sidedness, and completeness—yea, incalculableness—of its contents, brought with it no standard by which its own greatness could be measured: this standard, accordingly, had to be sought for extrinsically, and applied; and the whole motley army of those who came together with this common object—Jews and Christians, saints and sinners, orthodox fathers and heretics, councils and popes, reformers and protesters,—all of them, whether wishing doctrinally to expound or practically to apply the lessons of the Book, did it, consciously or unconsciously, in the method of Plato or Aristotle.

As with the peoples, so with the centuries,—we

find them under the headship of Aristotle and Plato, now in peaceful recognition, now in violent antagonism; and it is to be looked on as not the least favourable symptom of the present age, that it pays a willing and grateful homage to both these great men, as indeed, more than three centuries ago, the catholic appreciation of Raphael, in his school of Athens, had assigned to both sages their rightful place in the council of the wise.

Spinozism.

A Spinozistic cast of thought, which consorts well with the poetic instinct, the moment it is manipulated by reflection, becomes Machiavellism.

Prejudices.

The prejudices of men are rooted for the most part in their personal character; and on account of this close connection with the roots of personal existence, they cannot be removed. Neither evidence, nor understanding, nor reason, has the least effect on them.

Truth.

Truth is a torch, but a terrible one; oftentimes so terrible that the natural instinct of us all is to give a side-glance with a blinking eye, lest, looking it fairly in the face, the strong glare might blind us.

Men of Learning.

Learned men are generally hateful when they set themselves to the work of refutation. The man whose error employs them for the time they look upon as their mortal enemy.

German and Scotch Philosophy.

The reason why foreigners can make so little of our philosophy is simply this, that it has no direct relation to life. They cannot perceive what practical advantage they are to get from it, and for this reason they turn their attention more or less to the Scottish doctrine as it is set forth by Reid and Stewart. This doctrine has an affinity with the notions which guide men in ordinary life, and in this way acquires favour. It seems to reconcile the sensuous and the spiritual aspect of things, and to render possible the agreement of the real with the ideal, and thereby to bring about a more perfect state of human thinking and acting; and the very fact of its doing so, and holding forth such promises, gains for this school disciples and admirers.

Philology.

The confounding of one consonant with another might arise from an incapacity of the organs of speech; while the transformation of vowels into diphthongs might have been caused from some action of real or affected pathos.

Truth and Error.

Truth in certain regions runs counter to our nature; not so ERROR; and this from a very simple cause. The demand of truth frequently is, that we shall acknowledge our limitation; whereas error frequently fans in our souls the flattering conceit that in some favourite direction we may use unlimited sway, and all things be subject to our conception.

Analogy—Induction.

Thinking by analogy is not to be despised. Analogy has this merit, that it does not settle things—does not pretend to be conclusive. On the other hand, that *induction* is pernicious which, with a preconceived end in view, and working right forward for only that, drags in its train a number of unsifted observations, both false and true.

Self-delusion.

We are all so *borné*, as the French call it, so limited in our understandings, that we always believe that we are in the right; and so a man of great genius may readily exist who is not only wrong in important matters, but delights and revels in his wrongness.

Freedom from Error.

There is a sort of men who never go wrong, because they never propose to themselves anything reasonable to do.

Truth and Error.

It is much easier to recognise error than to discover truth; the one lies on the surface, and can be lightly picked up by a sharp eye; the other lies below, in depths which it is not every man's business to sound.

Spinoza.

I am reading Spinoza with Frau von Stein. I feel myself very near to him, though his soul is much deeper and purer than mine.

I cannot say that I ever read Spinoza straight through, that at any time the complete architecture of his intellectual system has stood clear in view before me. But when I look into him I seem to understand him—that is, he always appears to me consistent with himself, and I can always gather from him very salutary influences for my own way of feeling and acting.

Censoriousness.

It is always disagreeable when a man's self-esteem lets itself out in disparagement of others, even when they are very small men. A frivolous character may take his joke out of others, and treat them with every disrespect, just because he has no respect for himself. He who has learnt on solid grounds to put some value on himself, seems to have renounced the right of undervaluing others. And what are the best of us, that we should lift ourselves proudly above our brethren?

Freedom and Nature—Jacobi and Schelling— Knowledge and Love.

Jacobi's book against Schelling [1] was welcome to me, as helping me to realise the *statum controversiæ* between the champions of nature and those of freedom, which I had gone through with more or less completeness in my own experience. Nevertheless I must honestly confess that it gave me a sort of uncomfortable feeling. The truth is, that I am once for all the Ephesian goldsmith who have spent my whole life in the reverential contemplation of the great temple of the goddess, and in the artistic embodiment of her mysterious forms, and to whom it cannot possibly be an agreeable sensation when an

[1] Von den Göttlichen Dingen und ihrer Offenbarung, 1811.

apostle comes in upon me and insists upon forcing on me and my fellow-citizens a new god, and that a god without a form. Had I written a similar book in praise of the great Diana,—which, however, is not my business, because I belong to that class of men who love to live in peace, and not to stir up the people — but had I been moved to write such an apology,—I should have written on the reverse of the title-page, WE LEARN TO KNOW NOTHING BUT WHAT WE LOVE ; and the deeper we mean to penetrate into any matter with insight, the stronger and more vital must our love and passion be.

Knowledge.

I have been led to remark that a life full of activity and practice is scarcely sufficient to bring our knowledge to the highest point of purity and clearness. And yet to do this one thing only well—to acquire security and certainty in the appreciation of things exactly as they are, and to know them in their due subordination and in their proper relation to one another — this is really the highest enjoyment to which we ought to aspire, whether in the sphere of art, of nature, or of life.

Mathematics.

Mathematics, like dialectics, is an instrument of the inner higher understanding. Applied to practice, it becomes an art, like RHETORIC. In both these arts the form is everything, the substance nothing. To mathematics it is indifferent whether it reckons pence or pounds; to RHETORIC, whether it defends truth or falsehood.

MATHEMATICS can remove no prejudices and soften no obduracy. It has no influence in sweetening the bitter strife of parties; and in the moral world generally its action is perfectly null.

The mathematician is only in so far complete as he is a complete man, and feels within himself the beauty of truth. Then only will his work be profound, lucid, wise, genuine, pleasant, and even graceful. All this he must be, if he would be like La Grange.

Antiquity of Wisdom.

All truly wise thoughts have been thought already thousands of times; but to make them truly ours, we must think them over again honestly, till they take firm root in our personal experience.

Kant: Innate Ideas.

I agree with Kant's first sentence, that, though all our knowledge arises by occasion of experience, it does not therefore grow out of experience; further, in this, that no idea completely and in all points agrees with experience; nevertheless, idea and experience may be, or rather must be, in analogical correspondence.

Prophets.

Madman and dreamer they cried to Calchas, they
    cried to Cassandra,
Then when they sailed for Troy, then when from Troy
    they returned ;
Who will hear of to-morrow, when yesterday's lesson
    to mortals
Trumpet-tongued no man cares to remember to-day ?

The Whole and its Parts.

Wouldst comprehend the whole? then learn to scan
The parts : each part is parcel of the plan.

Or so,

Wouldst know the whole? then scan the parts; for all
That moulds the great lies mirrored in the small.

Show and Substance.

What show could be, unless of substance shown ;
And what were substance, if not shown to be?

Philosophy: its Upshot.

I'm open-eared to hear you, prophets, sages,
Poets and preachers, sounding through the ages;
I'm here to learn, but on this one condition,
That you be short, no big-mouthed exposition;
For all your wisdom, when I analyse it,
    Must mean but this—
To know the world, and yet not to despise it.

Truth.

Well, sir! I deem, the truth to tell,
    We never speak the truth completely;
But true with false compounded well
    Is the repast that tastes most sweetly.

Speculative Systems.

Weave your cobwebs in the sky!
    You're clever men, I don't deny it;
But in my lowly circle I
    Live my life, and profit by it.

Bird-Philosophy.

Seest thou the bird, how it flies from tree to tree of
    the orchard,
Hopping from branch to branch, pecking the pear
    and the plum?

Ask him, for he can discourse, and with eloquent
    prattle will tell you,
Verily he hath pierced nature's deep heart with his
    bill!

First Rule of Wisdom.

Use well the moment, and with seeing eyes
Peruse the thing that's next thee, and be wise!

Pre-established Harmony.

Were not a sun-like virtue in the eye,
It would not seek the sun that rules the sky;
And, were no God within to stir the brain,
The God without would speak to us in vain.

Liberty and Necessity.

Had God wished me to be a different man
From what I am, of spirit made and dust,
He would have made me on a different plan;
But, since I have the gift I have, I must
Use it with jealous care and holy trust.
I use it here, I use it there,
With what good fruit I scarcely know;
But, when my work of fruit is bare,
He'll say,—old bard, 'tis time to go!

Freedom and Necessity.

What happen must
Will happen. In quite common things, the will
And choice of men may triumph; but the highest
That rules our fate comes only God knows whence.

Love.

Nothing that is is stable. Many a jar
'Twixt man and man, the rolling seasons melt
By sweet gradations into harmony;
But that which bridges o'er the biggest gap
Is LOVE, whose charm binds topmost heaven to earth.

Logic.

Redeem the time, for fast it fleets away,
But order rules the hour it cannot stay.
Therefore 'tis plain that you must pass
First of all through the logic class.
There will your mind be postured rightly,
Laced up in Spanish buskins tightly,
That with caution and care, as wisdom ought,
It may creep along the path of thought,
And not with fitful flickering glow
Will-o'-the-wisp it to and fro.
There, too, if you hear the gentleman through
The term, to every lecture true,

You'll learn that a stroke of human thinking,
Which you had practised once as free
And natural as eating and drinking,
Cannot be made without one! two! three!
True, it should seem that the tissue of thought
Is like a web by cunning master wrought,
Where one stroke moves a thousand threads,
And one with the others thousand-fold weds:
Then steps the philosopher forth to show
How of need it must be so:
If the first be so, the second is so,
And therefore the third and the fourth is so;
And unless the first and the second before be,
The third and the fourth can never more be.
So schoolmen teach and scholars believe,
But none of them yet ever learned to weave.
He who strives to know a thing well
Must first the spirit within expel,
Then can he count the parts in his hand,
Only without the spiritual band.
Encheiresis naturæ, 'tis clept in Chemistry,
Thus laughing at herself, albeit she knows not why.

Nonsense.

Speak nonsense by the yard, or print
A book with nought but nonsense in't,

You'll break no bones ; with all your stir,
Things will remain just as they were.
But nonsense planted 'fore the eyes,
Hath glamour to confound the wise ;
It holds the sense with strong control,
And through the sense subdues the soul.

NATURE—NATURAL HISTORY

— — —

Wo fasse ich Dich, unendliche Natur?

NATURE—NATURAL HISTORY.

God and Nature.

THE contemplation of the architecture of the universe in the infinitely great and infinitely little of which it is composed, leads us inevitably to the conclusion that at the bottom of the whole an *idea* lies, according to which God in nature, and nature in God from eternity to eternity, works and shapes forth all things. Observation and reflection bring us continually nearer to these mysteries.

Physical Science: its Sphere and its Limits.

Every thinking man that looks at his almanac or his watch, will think with gratitude on the great master of science to whom he owes these most useful aids in the business of life. But allowing them all the regard that they may justly lay claim to in the domain of space and time, these mechanical aids must acknowledge that we, in our specially human sphere, are conscious of the existence of something that goes far beyond all contrivances of the kind, however cunning—something that is part of the universal and catholic heritage of humanity, and without which these curious helps would lose all grace of helping—viz., the IDEA, and LOVE.[1]

Flowers.

Flowers are the beautiful hieroglyphics of Nature, with which she indicates how much she loves us.

Natural History and Moral Science—Education.

The knowledge of nature is a good thing; but it must be studied primarily in its natural and healthy connection with ourselves. I would not force young people to court a curious intimacy with worms, and beetles, and monkeys, and other creatures removed from the natural range of human sympathy. With nature we should have nothing to do in the first place, except with so much of it as forms our living

[1] The use of the word *Idea* here is PLATONIC; *i.e.*, the great original thought of the Divine Being from which all the permanent types of things in this reasonable universe are shaped forth. Of this idea, man becomes partaker by virtue of his creation in the image of God, by the careful cherishing of the ideas which are ramifications of the original idea, and by sympathetic passion or love, which, as Goethe constantly emphasises, is the steam-power that sets all our cognitive machinery in healthy motion. Without love, the keenest and the most comprehensive intellect is merely a circular case of lancets, fit for nothing but cutting.—J. S. B.

environment. With every green tree whose rich leafage surrounds us, with every shrub on the roadside where we walk, with every grass that bends to the breeze in the field through which we pass, we have a natural relationship—they are our true compatriots. The birds that hop from twig to twig in our gardens, that sing in our bowers, are part of ourselves; they speak to us from our earliest years, and we learn to understand their language. Let a man ask himself, and he will find that every creature sundered from its natural surroundings, and brought into strange company, makes an unpleasant impression on us, which disappears only by habit. A man must live in a certain whirl of motley life before he can have any natural pleasure in apes, and parrots, and negro boys, and suchlike. If such odd and paradoxical creatures are to be studied in a healthy way, it must be in their native lands and amid their natural surroundings; and that master of natural science alone is worthy of respect who presents to us every creature, however strange and however odd, in its proper element and neighbourhood. Humboldt can so describe nature, and him I gladly hear.

A museum of natural history always seems to me like the tombs of Egyptian kings, in which various sorts of beasts and plants are preserved in mummified rigidity. These oddities may claim a curious attention from a caste of mystical priests; but into the sphere of general education such objects should never enter—not only as being out of place, but as in all likelihood displacing things which have better right to occupy the attention of the young. A teacher who tries to awaken the sympathetic interest of young persons in a single noble deed, or a single really good and heroic poem, does more towards his true growth than one who can tell off before him the names and describe the appearances of thousands of the inferior animals : for the upshot of all that curious study of low organisms is simply what we know already,—that man, and man alone, has in a peculiar and special sense been created in the image of God.

Individuals may be allowed to occupy themselves with natural objects and living creatures in the way that each may consider agreeable or useful; but always and everywhere the proper study of mankind is man.

The Typical Animal.

Experience best teaches the parts which are common to all animals : and in what respects these parts, though fundamentally the same, differ in each genus. Then abstraction comes in to classify the whole and construct a general scheme or type. This general type, which, of course, we have first to construct, and which it is our business as men of research to follow out in its minutest details, we shall find to be in the gross and scope of its presentation unchangeable; and even the highest classes of animals, not excluding the mammalia, will exhibit, under great diversity of form, a wonderful identity of fundamental type.

Physical Science.

A science, like every human creation and institution, is a Titanic structure of mingled false and true, of arbitrary and necessary. The common observations on nature and its procedure which we make from day to day, in whatever terms expressed, are really, after all, only *symptoms* which, if any real wisdom is to result from our studies, must be traced back to the physiological and pathological principles of which they are the exponents.

The Critical School and Nature.

SCHILLER and the Kantians are never tired of preaching the gospel of freedom; so be it: but only so that we do not ignore or overlook the absolute right of nature in certain matters. JACOBI, in his book on the things of God, uses the expression that "nature veils God": there is a meaning in this; but it is not for me, who have always been led by the force of an uncontrollable tendency, to see God in nature, and nature in God. What I see is not veiled.

Development.

When plants and animals are looked at in their first germs, it is almost impossible to distinguish them. A vital point, movable or half movable, is all that we can see, or scarcely see. Whether this rudimentary point is determinable on both sides, so as through the agency of light to be developed into the plant, or through darkness into an animal, we cannot say, although there are not wanting observations and analogies which point to this conclusion. But this much we may surely say, that the organisms which we know under the names of plants and animals, from the cradle of a scarce distinguishable relationship, by little and little usher themselves into day, become perfected in two opposite directions, in such fashion that the plant is glorified into the permanent stoutness and durability of the tree; while the animal mounts up to the perfection of mobility and freedom in man.

Specification.

Nature, in her process of specification, seems to get, so to speak, into a *cul de sac*, where she cannot advance, and whence she will not recede. Hence the persistency of national types of character.

Nature and Religion.

Assuredly there is no more lovely worship of God than that for which no image is required, but which springs up in our breast spontaneously, when nature speaks to the soul, and the soul speaks to nature face to face.

Nature—Observation—Systems.

Individual observations, drawn from the natural objects with which we are in contact, are often the more valuable, the less the observer professionally belongs to the particular department of science which he illustrates.

As soon as any one swears to a certain narrow creed in science, every unprejudiced and true perception is gone. The decided Vulcanist always sees through the spectacles of a Vulcanist; and every Neptunist, and every professor of the newest elevation theory, through his own. The contemplation of the world, with all these theorists who are devoted to an exclusive view, has lost its innocence, and the objects no longer appear in their natural purity.

Logic and Natural Science.

"Dialectics," said Hegel, "are in fact nothing more than the regulated, methodically cultivated spirit of contradiction which is innate in all men, and which shows itself great as a talent in the distinction between the true and false."

"Let us only hope," replied Goethe, "that these intellectual arts and dexterities are not frequently misused and employed to make the false true and the true false."

"That certainly happens," returned Hegel ; "but only with people who are mentally diseased."

"I therefore congratulate myself," said Goethe, "upon the study of nature, which preserves me from such a disease. For here we have to deal with the infinitely and eternally true, which throws off as incapable every one who does not proceed purely and honestly with the treatment and observation of his subject. I am also certain that many a dialectic disease would find a wholesome remedy in the study of nature."

Contemplation of Nature.

Spirit supreme ! thou gav'st me, gav'st me all,
For which I asked thee. Not in vain hast thou
Turned toward me thy countenance in fire.
Thou gavest me wide nature for my kingdom,
And power to feel it, to enjoy it. Not
Cold gaze of wonder gav'st thou me alone,
But even into her bosom's depth to look,
As it might be the bosom of a friend.
The grand array of living things thou mad'st

To pass before me : mad'st me know my brothers
In silent bush, in water, and in air.
And, when the straining storm loud roars and raves
Through the dark forest, and the giant pine
Root-wrenched tears all the neighbouring branches
    down,
And neighbouring stems, and strews the ground with
    wreck,
That to their fall the hollow mountain thunders ;
Then dost thou guide me to the cave, where safe
I learn to know myself, and from my breast
Deep and mysterious wonders are unfolded.

The Metamorphosis of Plants.

Why should it be, thou ask'st me well, so fair but to
    confound,
This garden rich, that spreads its breadth of broidered
    beauty round?
Names, learnèd names, thou hear'st, a host; a bar-
    barous-sounding train
They march, but still, as one comes in, the other
    leaves the brain.
And yet, belovèd, 'tis one truth, not complex, not
    profound,
One sacred simple truth, that rules this maze of tan-
    gled sound :

The ever-varying flowery forms, their thousands are
    but one;
There is a law that's like in all, but quite the same in
    none.
O my heart's chosen, if the thought that subtly stirs
    the brain,
Can teach the tongue, I'll tell thee now this law, nor
    tell in vain!
Behold the plant, by what nice rule, from the dark-
    groping root
Step after step it mounts the scale to blossom bright
    and fruit.
Behold the seed, the little seed, with silent plastic
    might,
How nurturing Earth the case unfolds, and to the
    genial light,
The ever-moving holy light, the delicate frame com-
    mends,
The slight, thin, leafy frame, that soon to gorgeous
    height ascends.
Simple the power slept in the seed; a nascent type is
    there
Of all that shall be, nicely wrapt, and swathed with
    curious care;
Half-formed and colourless, root and stem, leaflet and
    leaf there slept,
Their charmèd life all safe from harm by the arid
    kernel kept,

Till gentle dews and genial rain forth-draw the swelling might,
That shoots elastic from its bed of circumambient night.
But simple still the primal shoot; as in the boy the man,
Here lies of the full tree immense the unexpanded plan.
But mark, anon an impulse new, knot towered on knot behold!
And still as higher mounts the stalk, the primal type unrolled
Repeats itself; like, not the same; for in the leafy show
The upper floats with ampler pride than that which grew below.
More deeply cut, and cleft, and carved, and fringed in various trim,
The parts dispread, once closely twined in the inferior limb.
Thus step by step the growth proceeds, till perfect on the view
It bursts, a wonder ever old, a wonder ever new;
So giant-ribbed, so straggling free, in swelling breadth dilated,
As nature's self were weak to check the impulse she created.
But she is wise; and reining here the pride o' the leafy veins,
Gently prepares the crowning change, where perfect beauty reigns;

In narrower cells with milder pulse and calmer flow she lingers,
And soon the delicate frame displays the working of her fingers.
Back from the broad and leafy fringe the keen pulsation flows,
And buoyant now the topmost stem more light and graceful grows;
Leafless the tender stalklet's grace shoots eagerly on high,
And soon a shape of wonder bursts, and fills the studious eye.
Leaflet with leaflet trimly paired, the counted, the untold,
Rise, and, with nice adjustment ranged, their spreading wings unfold.
The parted cup unbinds its charge, and free in sunny ray
The million-coloured crowns aloft their blushing wealth display.
Thus Nature triumphs in her work, and in full glory shows
Each step i' the measured scale, through which to such fair height she rose;
And wonder still detains the eye, oft as the breeze-stirred blossom,
On delicate stalklet perched sublime, nods o'er the leafy bosom.

But not this gorgeous wealth remains : the strong creative power
Lives in the core; the hand divine stirreth the conscious flower,
And lo! with inward-curling force, each fine and slender thread
Elastic springs to find its mate, and with its like to wed :
And now they meet, the lovely pairs, and by a law divine,
In nuptial rings they stand around the consecrated shrine,
While Hymen hovers near, and wanton breezes odorous blow,
And clouds of genial dust forth roll, and vital fountains flow.
Asunder now, and cased apart, stands every swelling germ,
Soft-bosomed in the pulpy fruit, that shields its growth from harm ;
And Nature here the circle ends of her eternal working,
But still within the old the seed of a new life is lurking.
Link unto link she adds; that thus, as countless ages roll,
Part after part may share the pulse that stirs the mighty whole.

Look now, belovèd, on this web of broidered beauty round,
And feel it ne'er was woven thus so fair but to confound.
Each leafy plant thou seest declares the never-changing laws,
And every flower, loud and more loud, proclaims the Eternal Cause.
Nor here alone: once recognised the Godhead's mystic trace,
Thou'lt see through each most strange disguise the now familiar face;
In creeping grub, in wingèd moth, in various man thou'lt know
The one great soul that breathes beneath the curious-shifting show.
Bethink thee, then, how, in the hours that first together drew
Our hearts, from light acquaintance' germ familiar converse grew,
From converse sweet by gentle change how potent friendship rose,
Till perfect love within our breasts both flower and fruitage shows.
And this, bethink, what woven web of blest emotions grew,
Phase after phase of various love, the same but ever new!

And learn to enjoy the hour! pure love still upward
    strives to float
To that high sphere where wish to wish, and thought
    responds to thought,
Where feeling blent with feeling, raptures thrilled
    with raptures rare,
In bonds of a diviner life, unite the blissful pair.

Idem Latine redditum.

Te turbant, varii flores, te, vita, colores,
    Confundit picti copia multa soli?
Et, cum raucarum procedant agmina vocum,
    Nomina sed trudunt nomina rauca tamen.
Omnibus est species diversa, sed omnibus una est,
    Mystica lex flores sacraque norma regit.
Sit mihi, quam cupio, felix facundia linguæ,
    Arcanum ut possim pandere, vita, tibi.
Adspicias tenuis quam gestiat herba vigescens
    E teneris teneros elicuisse gradus.
Seminis e grano surgit, simul augmina lenta
    Prompserit e gravido gleba benigna sinu,
Mobilis ut tangat blanda irritamina lucis
    Frons tenera, inveniat lætificumque jubar.
Res simplex semen; perfectæ sed tamen herbæ,
    Intus erat species, implicitusque typus;
Frons, radix, germenque latent in semine parvo,
    Sed vaga forma tamen, sed color omnis abest.

Corticibus duris sic herba tenella tenetur,
  In sicco grano vita quieta sedet;
Donec lene madens turgescat semen, et ultro
  Emicet e densa nocte, petatque diem;
Sed simplex herbæ nascens manet usque figura,
  Sic puer est simplex, si quis adultus erit.
Jam culmum nova vis effert; mox augmine nodi
  Excipiunt nodos, et loca celsa petunt;
Sed simili semper formâ, variâ sed eâdem,
  Herba viget, primum pandere læta typum.
Jamque unâ frondes variantur imagine; jamque
  E glomere exserti per spatia ampla patent;
Pluribus et sectis iteratur partibus herba,
  Et frons in frondes finditur usque novas.
Sic amat in vastos arbor se pandere ramos
  Et multis (mirum!) luxuriare modis.
Naturam credas nullos sibi ponere fines,
  Ubere tam pleno magnificoque tumet.
Sed hic grata sibi sapiens moderamina figit,
  Et gradibus lentis egregiora petit;
Jam magis et placido tenuantur sanguine venæ,
  Jam tenuata viget tota figura magis.
Surgit dein gracilis sine fronde pedunculus; et mox
  Mirantem floris fabrica mira capit.
Nam petala in pulchrum vis vivida digerit orbem,
  Plurima, quæ numeres, quæ numeroque carent;
Cumque calix presso refugus se solverit axe,
  Panditur in plenum picta corona diem.

Sic splendet demum summo Natura triumpho
   Et gradibus cumulat leniter apta gradus;
Ut stupeas, iterumque novus stupor occupet ossa,
   Flos quoties summâ pendulus arce tremit.
Sed non usque manet prænuntia gloria floris;
   Quin genetrice dei tangitur ille manu,
Contrahiturque citus; tenui jam stamina filo
   Verticibus flexis fœdera sancta petunt;
Et jam cum pare par dulces irritat amores,
   Circumstatque aras fervida turba sacras;
Ipse Hymenæus adest, gratique feruntur odores,
   Sparsaque vitali pulvere fila rubent.
Jam se disjungunt; et germina singula turgent,
   Quæ tenero in gremio mollia poma tegunt.
Et hic vivificum genetrix vis conficit orbem,
   Excipit at sollers vincula rupta manus;
Scilicet ut longo producta propagine vivant
   Corpore cum toto singula membra simul.
Adspice nunc varios flores, nunc, vita, colores,
   Te turbat picti copia nulla soli;
Mystica nunc reserata patet lex sacraque norma,
   Clamat et ex herbis vox manifesta Dei.
Ast hic si pateat sacri tibi litera libri,
   Mutata specie, linea nota manet;
Sive eruca trahat larvam, seu papilionis
   Ala micet, vultus seu sibi mutet homo.
Sic nosterque accrevit amor; cognoscere vultus
   Fons erat; e dulci dulcior usus erat;

Vis et amicitiæ dein vinxit pectora ; donec
    Protulit et flores, pomaque firmus amor.
Hæc reputa ; reputa blandi solamina amoris
    Quot fuerint nobis, quam variata Venus.
Præsentemque diem liba ; sit et una voluntas
    Nobis—hic fructus summus amoris erit—
Unaque mens, ut quos dulcis concordia junxit
    Cum pare par læti regna serena petant.

ART

Bilde Künstler, rede nicht
Nur ein Hauch sey dein Gedicht

ART.

Beauty.

FROM Oeser I learned that the ideal of beauty consists in simplicity and repose—whence it plainly follows that no young man can produce a masterpiece. It is a great happiness when one has not had to arrive at this profound truth through a sad series of pretentious blunders.

The Line of Beauty.

Hogarth has given us the variations of the line of beauty from the extreme of distortion in living creatures to the phenomena of curvature in inorganic matter. The true point of the line of beauty is the LINE OF LOVE, having strength on the one side and weakness on the other. Love is the mean in which these extremes unite and produce perfection.

Beauty is at once the ultimate principle and the highest aim of art.

Art—Nature—Raphael.

The business of art is to give an external presentation of the natural. The purely natural, when it harmonises with our moral sentiments, is called *naïve*. The natural, of course, is always in one sense the real and the actual; but the actual is not always the natural. Apart from the moral sentiment, the actual is the common, the vulgar, the low, or the coarse.

The spirit of art is essentially noble; and therefore the great artist is never afraid of the low or the common, knowing, as he does, how to handle it nobly. He is an absolute sovereign, who has a right to show his sovereignty occasionally even in his whims. There is a spirit of daring, also, about a great genius, which loves to defy arbitrary restraints, and which will be gratified. Of all modern artists, Raphael is the most perfect. He is thoroughly *naïve;* with him the actual never comes into collision with the moral or the holy. In the most sacred compositions, he can bring in Moors and monkeys playing with apples on a camel's back—a whole world of the lowest, without anyhow trenching on the highest.

Humour in Art.

Humour is one of the elements of genius, admirable as an adjunct, but as soon as it becomes dominant, only a surrogate for genius. Humour in this illegitimate form accompanies the decline of art, corrupts it, and then destroys it.

Head-knowledge.

Unless the heart is in perfect and continuous sympathy with the head, the comprehension of any work of art is impossible.

Art and the Public.

The public is large : true judgment, true feeling, are not quite so rare as one believes ; only the artist ought not to demand an unconditional approval of his work. Unconditional approval is always the least valuable ; conditional those who are eager for approval are seldom content with. In life, as in art, I know well a person must take counsel with himself when he purposes to do or to produce anything ; but when it is produced or done, he must listen with attention to the voices of a number, and with a little practice, out of these many votes he will be able to collect a perfect judgment. The few who could themselves pronounce one, for the most part hold their peace.

Art and Imitation.

Imitation is born with us. What should be imitated is not easy to discover. The excellent is rarely found, more rarely valued. The height charms us, the steps to it not so; with the summit in our eyes, we love to walk along the plain. It is but a part of art that can be taught; the artist needs the whole. Who knows the half speaks much, and is always wrong; who knows the whole inclines to act, and speaks seldom or late. The former have no secrets and no force; the instruction they can give is like baked bread, savoury and satisfying for a single day; but flour cannot be sown, and seed-corn ought not to be ground.

Music.

Music is sacred or profane. Sacred music is that species which is most completely in accordance with the dignity of the art, and has the greatest influence upon life—an influence which is exercised over a much greater range of ages and epochs than to the other arts can belong; of the profane or secular species, cheerfulness should always be the dominant characteristic.

Painting.

Painting is of all the arts the one which may be taken most lightly and easily. The reason of this lies in the material and objects with which it works. Then again, we must consider that a skilful piece of drawing, though utterly destitute of genius, commands admiration alike from the cultivated and the uncultivated. Here truthfulness in the colours, surfaces, and natural selection of visible objects is pleasant; and besides, as the eye anyhow is accustomed to look on both fair and foul, a deformity, even an abortion, is not so offensive to it as a discord to the ears. We set some value on the worst drawing, because we are accustomed to see much worse things in reality. The painter, accordingly, needs only to be to some small extent an artist, and he finds forthwith a greater audience, who stand on the same level with him, than does the musician. And in many cases a painter, however feeble in genuine artistic instinct, can work by himself; whereas the inferior musician must associate himself with others, in order that he may produce some effect by acting in concert with them.

What and How.

The WHAT in a work of art interests men more than the *how:* that they can appropriate in detail; this they cannot grasp as a whole. Hence comes the habit of dwelling on particular passages, along with which, no doubt, the total impression comes so far into play, though quite unconsciously to the approving critic.

Art and Inspiration.

To blow is not to play the flute; the fingers must command the stops.

An Æsthetical Whole.

Few men of any modern nation have a proper sense of an æsthetical whole : they praise and blame by parts ; they are charmed by passages ; and who has greater reason to rejoice in this than actors, since the stage is ever but a patched and piecemeal matter ?[1]

Art and Nature.

In nature we never see anything isolated, but everything in connection with something else which is before it, beside it, under it, and over it. A single object, I grant, may strike us as particularly picturesque : it is not, however, the object alone which produces this effect, but it is the connection in which we see it, with that which is beside, behind, and above it, all of which contributes to that effect.

Thus during a walk I may meet with an oak, the picturesque effect of which surprises me. But if I represent it alone, it will perhaps no longer appear to me as it did, because that is wanting which contributed to and enhanced the picturesque effect in nature. Thus, too, a wood may appear beautiful through the influence of one particular sky, one particular light, and one particular situation of the sun. But if I omit all these in my drawing, it will perhaps

---

[1] Compare here the speech of the manager in the *Vorspiel* to Faust, beginning " Besonders aber lass genug geschehen."

appear without any force, and as something indifferent to which the proper charm is wanting. Further, there is in nature nothing beautiful which is not produced (*motivirt*) as true in conformity with the laws of nature. In order that that truth of nature may appear true also in the picture, it must be accounted for by the introduction of the influential circumstances.

I find by a brook well-formed stones, the parts of which, exposed to the air, are in a picturesque manner covered with green moss. Now it is not alone the moisture of the water which has caused this formation of moss; but perhaps a northerly aspect, or the shade of the trees and bushes, that has co-operated in this formation at this part of the brook. If I omit these influential causes in my picture, it will be without truth, and without the proper convincing power.

Thus the situation of a tree, the kind of soil beneath it, and other trees behind and beside it, have a great influence on its formation. An oak which stands exposed to the wind on the western summit of a rocky hill, will acquire quite a different form from that of one which grows below on the moist ground of a sheltered valley. Both may be beautiful in their kind, but they will have a very different character, and can, therefore, in an artistically conceived landscape, be used only for such a situation as they occupied in nature. And, therefore, the delineation of surrounding objects, by which any particular situation is expressed, is of high importance to the artist. On the other hand, it would be foolish to attempt to represent all those prosaic casualties which have had as little influence upon the form of the principal object as upon its picturesque effect for the moment.

Art: a Subject.

What can be more important than the subject, and what is all the science of art without it? All talent is wasted, if the subject is unsuitable. It is because modern artists have no worthy subjects that people are so hampered in all the art of these times. I myself have not been able to renounce my modernness. Very few artists are clear on this point. For instance, they paint my "Fisherman" as the subject of a picture, and do not think that it cannot be painted. In this ballad nothing is attempted, but that charm in water which tempts me to bathe in summer—and how can that be painted?

Mannerism.

Mannerism is always longing to have done, and has no true enjoyment in work. A genuine really great talent, on the other hand, has its greatest happiness in execution. Roos, for instance, is unwearied in drawing the hair and wool of his goats and sheep; and you see by his infinite details that he enjoyed the purest felicity in doing his work, and had no wish to bring it to an end.

Inferior talents do not enjoy art for its own sake; while at work they have nothing before their eyes but the profit they hope to make when they have done. With such worldly views and tendencies nothing great was ever produced.

Religion and Art.

I talked of the mistake of those artists who make religion art, while for them art should rather be a religion. Religion, we agreed, stands in the same relation to art as any other of the higher interests in life. It is merely to be looked on as a material, with similar claims to any other vital material. Faith and want of faith are not the organs with which a work of art is to be apprehended. On the contrary, human powers and capacities of a totally different character are required. Art must address itself to those organs with which we apprehend it; otherwise it misses its effect. A religious material may be a good subject for art, but only in so far as it possesses general human interest. The Virgin with the Child is on this account an excellent subject, and one that may be treated a hundred times, and always seen again with pleasure.

Love of Display in Art.

The misfortune is that nobody cares to enjoy what has been produced by others, but every one wants to reproduce on his own account. There is, besides, no earnestness to approach the whole, no willingness to do anything for the sake of the whole; but each one tries to make his own self observable, and to exhibit it as much as possible to the world. This false tendency is shown everywhere, and people imitate the modern musical *virtuosi*, who do not select those pieces which give the audience pure musical enjoyment, so much as those in which they can gain admiration by the dexterity they have acquired. Everywhere there is the individual who wants to show himself off to advantage—nowhere the honest effort to make himself subservient to the whole.

Beauty and Nature.

"I cannot help laughing at the æsthetical folks," said Goethe, "who torment themselves in endeavouring, by some abstract terms, to reduce to a conception that inexpressible thing to which we give the name of beauty. Beauty is a primeval phenomenon, which never makes an independent appearance, but the reflection of which is visible in a thousand different utterances of the creative mind, and is as various as Nature herself."

"I have often heard it said that Nature is always beautiful," said I; "that she causes the artists to despair, because they are seldom capable of reaching her completely."

"Nature," said Goethe, "in many of her works reveals a charm of beauty which no human art can hope to reach; but I am by no means of opinion that she is beautiful in all her aspects. Her intentions are indeed always good, but not so the conditions which are required to make her manifest herself completely.

"Thus, the oak is a tree which may be very beautiful; but how many favourable circumstances must concur before Nature can succeed in producing one truly beautiful? If an oak grow in the midst of a forest, encompassed with large neighbouring trunks, its tendency will be always upwards, towards free air and light; only small weak branches will grow on its sides, and these will in the course of a century decay and fall off. But if it has at last succeeded in reaching the free air with its summit, it will then rest in its upward tendency, and begin to spread itself from its sides and form a crown. But it is by this time already passed its middle age, its many years of upward striving have consumed its freshest powers, and its present endeavour to put forth its strength by increasing in breadth will not now have its proper results. When full grown, it will be high, strong, and slender-stemmed, but still without such a proportion between its crown and its stem as would render it beautiful.

"The main point," continued Goethe, "is that the race be pure, and that man have not applied his mutilating hand. A horse with its mane and tail cut, a hound with cropped ears, a tree from which the strongest branches have been lopped and the rest cut into a spherical form, and above all, a young girl whose youthful form has been spoiled and deformed by stays, are things from which good taste revolts, and which merely occupy a place in the Philistine's catechism of beauty."

Schools of Art.

A school of art, or of anything else, is to be looked on as a single individual, who keeps talking to himself for a hundred years, and feels an extreme satisfaction with his own circle of favourite ideas, be they ever so silly.

Modern Art.

In the present advanced state of art productions are possible which are null, and yet not bad : null because they have no contents; not bad because the artist worked under the influence of good models, which bring execution generally up to a certain level of excellence.

Portrait-Painters.

Portrait-painters are a class of artists for whom I have always felt great pity. Seldom or never does it happen that one is content with the portrait of a person with whom he is intimately acquainted. What we are not accustomed to demand from other persons, that we are forward to demand from portrait-painters — the impossible. They are expected to put into their picture whatever this spectator or the other, from his peculiar point of view, may expect to find in the likeness; they are called upon to represent not only the man as they may happen to see him, but as anybody may happen to have seen him. I am therefore not at all surprised, when I find, as I often do, that such artists become unimpressible, indifferent, and obstinate.

Palladio.

The more Palladio is studied, the more incalculable will appear the genius, the mastery, the wealth, the versatility, and the grace of this man.

Training and Discipline.

Few feelings are more pleasant than that of having, by good advice or otherwise, contributed to the scientific training of a fine natural genius; and friendly help of this kind is more important at the present day than in the old times, when every beginner started with a firm faith in the school and in the rules of his art, and willingly submitted himself to whatever drudgery might belong to the grammar of his profession—a submission of which the aspiring young artist of the present day generally will know nothing. The German artists, these thirty years back, are living in the conceit that a happy genius can train itself; and a host of passionate admirers and amateurs, equally destitute of all solid foundation, are at hand to confirm them in this delusion. How often have I not heard the praise of a young artist trumpeted in these terms—*he owes everything to himself?* This I hear for the most part with all patience; but now and then I add sharply — *and his work is accordingly.*

Ideality—Claude Lorraine.

Claude Lorraine knew the real world down to its minutest details; and he used it as the means to express to the world his own beautiful soul. And this indeed is true *ideality*—the ideality which loves to make use of the *material* presented to it by nature in such a fashion that, the ideal truth thus embodied, the matter and the spirit, is accepted as the *actual.*

Personality.

In art and poetry personal genius is everything; yet we have seen amongst modern critics and connoisseurs certain persons not of the strongest type of intellect, who will have it that in a great work of art the personality of the artist is only a small adjunct in the great result. But the fact is, in the great work the great person is always present as the great factor; only, to appreciate the presence of a great somebody in any work of genius, the person who would appreciate must himself be a somebody.

Training and Discipline.

I said that I had lately, in his 'Italian Travels,' read of a picture by Correggio, which represents a "weaning," and in which the infant Christ in Mary's lap stands in doubt between His mother's breast and a pear held before Him, and does not know which of the two to choose.

"Ay," said Goethe, "there is a little picture for you! There are mind, *naïveté*, sensuousness, all together. The sacred subject is endowed with a universally human interest, and stands as a symbol for a period of life we must all pass through. Such a picture is immortal, because it grasps backwards at the earliest times of humanity, and forward at the latest. On the contrary, if Christ were painted suffering the little children to come unto Him, it would be a picture that expressed nothing — at any rate, nothing of importance."

Art and Practice.

Practice and habit must in every art fill up the voids which genius and temper in their fluctuations will so often leave.

Art and Nature.

I have never observed nature with a view to poetical production; but because my early drawing of landscapes, and my later studies in natural science, led me to a constant, close observation of natural objects, I have gradually learned nature by heart, even to the minutest details; so that, when I need anything as a poet, it is at my command, and I cannot easily sin against truth. Schiller had not this observation of nature. The localities of Switzerland, which he used in "William Tell," were all related to him by me; but he had such a wonderful mind, that even from hearsay he could make something that possessed reality.

We say to the artist, Study nature! But it is not such an easy matter from the trivial to eliminate the noble, and from the amorphous to conjure out the beautiful.

Art—the Dilettante.

It is the very nature of the *dilettanti* that they have no idea of the difficulties which lie in a subject, and always wish to undertake something for which they have no capacity.

Art and Superstition.

Superstition is part of the poetry of life; therefore superstition can do the artist no harm.

Art: its completeness.

A work of art will always be defective when any of the functions that go to make a complete man have not presided at its production. The abysses of presentiment, a clear and firm intuition of the present, mathematical depth, physical accuracy, height of reason, sharpness of understanding, a quick and fervid fancy, a loving joy in the natural and healthy delights of the senses, no faculty and no function can be dispensed with, if that fruitful and profitable mastery of the moment is to take place, out of which alone a work of art of whatsoever character can spring into existence.

Art and Religion.

Art rests on a sort of religious sense, or a deep-rooted earnestness of character; and this earnestness it is which so readily leads it to form a union with religion. Religion, on the other hand, requires no feeling for art; it rests on its own basis; and neither imparts artistic inspiration nor even cultivates taste.[1]

---

[1] The most striking example of this is in Scotland, where a form of extreme Protestantism, founded on rigid dogmatism and fervid moral earnestness, assumed an attitude, the natural result of a historical development, positively hostile to all æsthetical culture. But this unnatural divorce between the holy and the beautiful, aided by various softening influences of the present century, is fast receding from the sympathy of the more cultivated classes in this country.—J. S. B.

Art and Human Nature.

Man is not only a thinking, he is also a feeling animal. He is a whole, a unity of many wonderfully connected powers; and to this complex unity, not in its parts, but as a whole, every work of art must address itself; corresponding, like the chord in music, to the rich unity, and the curiously unified manifoldness of which human nature is made up.

Real and Ideal.

The bird flies in the air with proper zest
When it looks down upon an earthly nest.

Unity in Multiplicity.

For evermore exists the one, that still
Is branched into the many, and still is one,
And one that knows no second. For the one
Find thou the many, and feel the many as one,
And thou hast learned where all true art begins,
And where it ends.

Silent Work.

Artist, let thy words be few,
To thy shaping tool be true,
And work thy soul from day to day,
Like a breath into the clay!

Art and Religion—Diana of the Ephesians.

At Ephesus a goldsmith sate
In his workshop working stoutly,
What best he could, both air and late,
With practised hand devoutly.
He from a boy ofttime had knelt
Before the great Diana's shrine;
Ofttime at home with fingers fine
Had chased the curious-figured belt,
With strange wild beasts of every kind
Beneath her nurturing breast to bind,
Well pleased his talent to employ
Even as the father taught his boy;
And now a master grown, he plied
His father's art with pious pride.

One day as he worked at his job
He heard a cry from a noisy mob,
Saying that only one God did reign,
Somewhere fancied, nowhere seen,
At the back of a silly mortal's brain,—
The true God this, not his great queen,
That peoples with life earth's wide domain.

He quietly bade his men go out,
To see what all the noise was about,
And then went on with his graving-tool
With stags and hounds to fill the space

About the knee, according to rule;
Then prayed to Pallas for her good grace
To top the form with a worthy face.

Thus he; and you, a man of pith,
Of course are free to choose your creed;
Swear by what god may help your need,
But leave Diana to the smith.[1]

Good Advice.

There comes a day with you and me
When all things with us disagree;
We hate ourselves, our friends we hate,
And doubt all good, and rail at fate.
Now, if in life such things may be,
Should ART from all ill lunes be free?
Therefore, when you're not in the vein,

---

[1] In this poem, as in the "Bride of Corinth" and others, Goethe has shown how well he can appreciate the polytheistic point of view; this appreciation is the result of the many-sided sympathy which belonged to his rich human nature. It seems to prove also, no doubt, that if he had lived at Ephesus when the Gospel was preached there, his artistic instincts would have led him to prefer the old physico-æsthetical truth that lay in Cybele to the new moral truth that was preached in the name of Christ; but to conclude from this, as some have done, that he did not now appreciate what Christianity has done for the world, would be illegitimate, and lead to an inference contradicted not only by many distinct utterances in his works, but founded on a total misconception of the mental constitution of the man. —J. S. B.

Omit to spur the jaded brain;
The tide that ebbs will flow again;
From rest to-day you wisely borrow
A double strength to bless to-morrow.

Taste and Genius.

Taste and genius, why do they never pull kindly together?
Taste is afraid of the power, genius spurneth the rein.

Grace and Strength.
(To a Skater.)

Wouldst thou be deft in thy wheeling, first learn to be firm in thy footing;
Only from fulness of strength Grace may be born to the light.

WOMEN

Die Sittlichkeit umgibt mit einer Mauer
Das zarte leicht verletzliche Geschlecht.

WOMEN.

The Model Wife.

To the man who knows the world, who understands what he should do in it, what he should hope from it, nothing can be more desirable than meeting with a wife who will everywhere co-operate with him; who will everywhere prepare his way for him; whose diligence takes up what his must leave; whose occupation spreads itself on every side, while his must travel forward on its single path. What a heaven had I figured for myself beside Theresa! Not the heaven of an enthusiastic bliss, but of a sure life on earth; order in prosperity, courage in adversity, care for the smallest, and a spirit capable of comprehending and managing the greatest. Oh, I saw in her the qualities which, when developed, make such women as we find in history, whose excellence appears to us far preferable to that of men: this clearness of view; this expertness in all emergencies; this sureness in details, which brings the whole so accurately out, although they never seem to think of it.

Love.

Alas! she was not lovely when she loved; the greatest misery which can befall a woman.

Women and Children.

What in us the women leave uncultivated, children cultivate, when we retain them near us.

Women—Mothers.

Nothing is more charming than to see a mother with a child upon her arm; nothing is more reverend than a mother among many children.

Woman's Sphere—The Family Home.

And where is there any station higher than the ordering of the house? While the husband has to vex himself with outward matters; while he has to gather wealth and to protect it; while perhaps he takes a share in the administration of the state, and there constantly depends on circumstances, ruling nothing, I may say, while he conceives that he is ruling much, compelled to be only politic where he would willingly be reasonable, to dissemble where he would be open, to be false where he would be upright; while thus, for the sake of an object which he never reaches, he must every moment sacrifice the first of objects, harmony with himself,—a reasonable housewife is actually governing in the interior of her family; has the comfort and activity of every person in it to provide for and make possible. What is the highest happiness of us mortals, if not to execute what we consider right and good; to be really masters of the means conducive to our aims? And where should or can our first and nearest aims be but within the house? All those indispensable and still-to-be-renewed supplies, where do we expect, do we require to find them, if it is not in the place where we arise and where we go to sleep,—where kitchen and cellar, and every species of accommodation for ourselves and ours, are to be always ready? What unvarying activity is needed to conduct this constantly recurring series in unbroken living order! How few are the men to whom it is given to return regularly like a star; to command their day as they command their night; to form for themselves their household instruments; to sow and to reap, to gain and to expend, and to travel round their circle with perpetual success and peace and love! It is when a woman has attained this inward mastery, that she truly makes the husband, whom she loves, a master: her attention will acquire all sorts of knowledge for her; her activity will turn them all to profit. Thus is she dependent upon no one; and she procures her husband genuine independence, that which is interior and domestic: whatever he possesses he beholds secured—what he earns, well employed; and thus he can direct his mind to lofty objects, and if fortune favours, he may act in the state the same character which becomes his wife so well at home.

Marriages.

It is interior disagreements only that affright me; a frame that does not fit what it is meant to hold; much pomp and little real enjoyment; wealth and avarice, nobility and rudeness, youth and pedantry, poverty and ceremonies, these are the things which would annihilate me, however it may please the world to stamp and rate them.

Wives.

Indeed men's understandings give their suffrages for household wives; but their hearts and their imaginations long for other qualities; and we housekeeping people can ill stand a rivalry with the beautiful and the lovely.

Marriages—Suitable and Unsuitable.

Nothing gives a greater loose to people's tongues, than when a marriage happens which they can denominate unsuitable: and yet the unsuitable are far more common than the suitable; for, alas! with most marriages, it is not long till things assume a very piteous look. The confusion of ranks by marriage can be called unsuitable, only when the one party is unable to participate in the manner of existence, which is native, habitual, and which at length grows absolutely necessary, to the other. The different classes have different ways of living, which they cannot change or communicate to one another; and this is the reason why connections such as these in general were better not be formed. Yet exceptions, and exceptions of the happiest kind, are possible. Thus, too, the marriage of a young woman with a man advanced in life is generally unsuitable; yet I have seen some such turn out extremely well. For me, I know but of one kind of marriage that would be entirely unsuitable; that in which I should be called upon to make a show and manage ceremonies: I had rather give my hand to the son of any honest farmer in the neighbourhood.

Marriage.

He who attacks marriage, he who by word or deed sets himself to undermine this foundation of all moral society, he must settle the matter with me; and if I don't bring him to reason, then I have nothing to do with him. Marriage is the beginning and the summit of all civilisation. It makes the savage mild; and the most highly cultivated man has no better means of demonstrating his mildness. Marriage must be indissoluble, for it brings so much general happiness, that any individual case of unhappiness that may be connected with it cannot come into account.

What do people mean when they talk about unhappiness? It is not so much unhappiness as impatience that from time to time possesses men, and then they choose to call themselves miserable. Let the moment of irritation but pass over, and people will find cause enough to think themselves happy that a state which has already existed so long still exists. For separation there can be no sufficient reason. In our present human condition there is so much of sorrow and joy interwoven, that it is beyond all calculation what obligations a married pair lie under to one another. It is an infinite debt which it requires an eternity to cancel. Disagreeable it may be, I admit, sometimes: that is just as it should be. Are we not really married to our conscience, of which we might often be willing to rid ourselves because it often annoys us more than any man or woman can possibly annoy one another?

Wisdom of Women.

A noble man is by a well-dropt word
Of women wisely led.

Women.

If thou wouldst hear what seemly is and fit,
Inquire of noble women; they can tell;
Who in life's common usage hold their place
By graceful deed, and aptly chosen word.
Propriety as with a wall surrounds
Their delicate sense, which shrinks from forward
  touch,
And where rude handling is no woman lives:
Ask both the sexes, both have one reply—
For freedom he, and she for chaste restraint.

Woman: her Persistency.

Pity sits throned with woman. For a man
The best that is will train his heart to look
On savage deeds unmoved, and what at first
He hated, end by honouring as a law,
Till monstered from boon nature's use he grows
Into a thing scarce human. But a woman
Lives to herself, as her pure purpose shaped,
In singleness of heart. For good or ill
She is to-day what she was yesterday
And will remain to-morrow.

Woman.

I would not blame the gods; but sooth to say,
The state of womankind is pitiful:

At home and in the camp the man is master,
And cast abroad he knows to fight his way.
Possessions, honour, victory, are his;
And, when he dies, he dies as heroes die.
But woman, oh, within what narrow cirque
Her fate is bounded! an unfeeling lord
With meek submissive service to obey
Is her mere duty; and divorced from home
She wanders like a waif upon the wave
Unfriended.

EDUCATION AND CULTURE

Unsere zweideutige zertreute Erziehung macht den Menschen ungewiss; sie erregt Wünsche, statt Triebe zu beleben.

EDUCATION AND CULTURE.

Education.

NOTHING is worse than a teacher who knows only as much as he has to impart to the hearer. He who would teach others may oftentimes wisely suppress the best of what he knows; but he must not deal in half-knowledge. Well, but you will ask, Where are such teachers to be found? The answer is easy. Go to the place where the thing you wish to know is native; your best teacher is there. Where the thing you wish to know is so dominant that you must breathe its very atmosphere, there teaching is most thorough, and learning is most easy. You acquire a language most readily in the country where it is spoken; you study mineralogy best among miners; and so with everything else.

Utility.

The use of a thing is only a part of its significance. To know anything thoroughly, to have the full command of it in all its applications, we must study it on its own account, independently of any special application.

The Beginning.

All beginning is difficult, says the proverb. True enough, no doubt, in a certain sense; but with a more comprehensive truth one can say, *All beginning is easy;* and the highest steps on the ladder are the most difficult to reach.

The Best Education.

The best type of education is that of the Hydriotes. As islanders and seamen they take their children with them from their earliest years into the ship, and let them creep their way up, from stage to stage of the naval art. As soon as they are able to do substantial service, they are allowed their share in the profits of the trade; and in this way is formed a class of persons who are at once the most daring seamen and the most successful merchants. In such a school the naval heroes are bred, who sail up in their fire-ship right upon the admiral's ship of the foe, and grapple with it hand to hand.

The True Scholar.

The true scholar learns to develop the unknown from the known, and thus step by step approaches to the platform of his master.

Early Impressions.

"Let no one think that he can conquer the first impressions of his youth. If he has grown up in enviable freedom, surrounded with beautiful and noble objects, in constant intercourse with worthy men; if his masters have taught him what he needed first to know, for comprehending what remained more easily; if he has never learned anything which he requires to unlearn; if his first operations have been so guided, that, without altering any of his habits, he can more easily produce what is excellent in future;—then such a one will lead a purer, more perfect, and happier life, than another man who has wasted the force of his youth in opposition and error. A great deal is said and written about education; yet I meet with very few who can comprehend and transfer to practice the simple yet vast idea, which includes within itself all others connected with the subject."

"That may well be true," said Wilhelm; "for the generality of men are limited enough in their conceptions to suppose that every other should be fashioned by education according to the pattern of themselves. Happy, then, are those whom fate takes charge of, and educates according to their several natures!"

"Fate," said the other, smiling, "is an excellent but most expensive schoolmaster. In all cases I would rather trust to the reason of a human tutor.

Fate, for whose wisdom I entertain all imaginable reverence, often finds in Chance, by which it works, an instrument not over-manageable. At least the latter very seldom seems to execute precisely and correctly what the former had determined."

"You seem to express a very singular opinion," said Wilhelm.

"Not at all!" replied the other. "Most part of what happens in the world confirms my opinion. Do not many incidents at their commencement show some mighty meaning, and generally terminate in something paltry?"

"You mean to jest."

"And as to what concerns the individual man," pursued the other, "is it not so with him likewise? Suppose Fate had appointed one to be a good player; and why should it not provide us with good players as well as other good things? Chance might conduct the youth into some puppet-show perhaps, where, at such an early age, he could not help taking interest in what was tasteless and despicable, reckoning insipidities endurable or even pleasing, and thus corrupting and misdirecting his primary impressions —impressions which can never be effaced, and whose influence, in spite of all our efforts, cling to us in some degree to the very last."

"What makes you think of puppet-shows?" said Wilhelm, not without some consternation.

"It was an accidental instance; if it does not

please you, we shall take another. Suppose Fate had appointed any one to be a great painter, and it pleased Chance that he should pass his youth in sooty huts, in barns and stables; do you think that such a man would ever be enabled to exalt himself to purity, to nobleness, to freedom of soul? The more keenly he may in his youth have seized on the impure, and tried in his own manner to ennoble it, the more powerfully in the remainder of his life will it be revenged on him; because, while he was endeavouring to conquer it, his whole being has become inseparably combined with it. Whoever spends his early years in mean and pitiful society, though at an after period he may have the choice of better, will yet constantly look back with longing towards that which he enjoyed of old, and which has left its impression blended with the memory of all his young and unreturning pleasures."

Education—Universities.

They teach in universities far too many things, and far too much that is useless. Then the individual professors extend their department too much, far beyond the wants of their hearers. In former days lectures were read in chemistry and botany as belonging to medicine, and the physician could manage them. Now, both these have become so extensive, that each of them requires a lifetime; yet acquaintance with both is expected from the physician. Nothing can come of this: one thing must be neglected and forgotten for the sake of the other. He who is wise puts aside all claims which may dissipate his attention, and confining himself to one branch, excels in that.

Completeness of Culture.

"It is all men that make up mankind; all powers taken together that make up the world. These are frequently at variance: and as they endeavour to destroy each other, Nature holds them together by various devices, and again produces them in their diversity. From the first animal tendency to handicraft attempts, up to the highest practising of intellectual art; from the inarticulate tones and crowings of the happy infant, up to the polished utterance of the orator and singer; from the first bickerings of boys up to the vast equipments by which countries are conquered and retained; from the slightest kindliness and the most transitory love, up to the fiercest passion and the most earnest covenant; from the merest perception of sensible presence, up to the faintest presentiments and hopes of the remotest spiritual future;—all this, and much more also, lies in man, and must be cultivated: yet not in one, but in many. Every gift is valuable, and ought to be unfolded. If one encourages the beautiful alone, and another encourages the useful alone, it takes them both to form a man. The useful encourages itself; for the multitude produce it, and no one can dispense with it: the beautiful must be encouraged; for few can set it forth, and many need it."

"One power rules another; but no power can cultivate another: in each endowment, and not elsewhere, lies the force which must complete it: this many people do not understand, who yet attempt to teach and influence. . . . Let us merely keep a clear and steady eye on what is in ourselves; on what endowments of our own we mean to cultivate: let us be just to others; for we ourselves are only to be valued, in so far as we know to value our brother."

Conventional Morality.

Oh needless strictness of morality! while Nature in her own kindly manner trains us to all that we require to be. Oh strange demands of civil society, which first perplexes and misleads us, then asks of us more than Nature herself! Woe to every sort of culture which destroys the most effectual means of all true culture, and directs us to the end, instead of rendering us happy on the way!

Culture.

The rude man is contented, if he see but something going on; the man of more refinement must be made to feel; the man of true culture desires to reflect.

Balance of Culture.

It is with the cultivation of an artistic as with the cultivation of every other talent. Our strong points to a certain extent develop themselves; but those capacities of our nature which are not in daily exercise, and are therefore less vigorous, need particular care, in order that they likewise may become strong, and contribute their share to the general balance of the organism.

So may a young singer possess certain natural tones which are very excellent, and which leave nothing to desire; while other tones in his voice may be found less strong, clear, and full. But these are the very tones which he by constant exercise must seek to bring to equal perfection with the others.

The Commonplace.

Men are so inclined to content themselves with what is common—the spirit and the senses so easily grow dead to the impressions of the beautiful and perfect—that every one should study to nourish in his mind the faculty of feeling the best things by every method in his power. For no man can bear to be entirely deprived of such enjoyments; it is only because they are not used to taste of what is excellent, that so many people take delight in silly and insipid things, provided they be new. For this reason one ought every day at least to hear a pleasant song, read a good poem, see a fine picture, and, if it be possible, speak a few reasonable words.

Culture.

Every cultivated person knows how keenly he has to contend against a certain rudeness both in others and in himself; how much his culture costs him; how apt he is after all, in certain cases, to think of himself alone, forgetting what he owes to others. How often has a worthy person to reproach himself with having failed to act with proper delicacy! And when a fine nature too delicately, too conscientiously, cultivates, nay, if you will, over-cultivates itself, there seems to be no toleration, no indulgence for it in the world. Yet such persons are, without us, what the ideal of perfection is within us; models not for being imitated, but for being aimed at.

Examinations.

I cannot approve of the requisition in the studies of future statesmen, of so much theoretically learned knowledge, by which young people are often ruined before their time, both in mind and body. When they enter into practical life, they possess indeed an immense stock of philosophical and learned material; but in the narrow circle of their calling this cannot be practically applied, and will therefore be forgotten as useless. On the other hand, what they most needed they have lost; they are deficient in the necessary mental and bodily energy which is quite indispensable when one would enter with efficiency into practical life.

And then, are not love and benevolence also needed in the life of a statesman—in the management of men? And how can any one feel and exercise benevolence towards another, when he is ill at ease in his own skin?

The Art of Teaching.

To guard from error is not the instructor's duty, but to lead the erring pupil; nay, to let him quaff his error in deep satiating draughts is sometimes his best wisdom. He who only tastes his error will long dwell with it, will take delight in it as in a singular felicity; while he who drains it to the dregs will, if he be not crazy, find it to be what it is.

Education—Discipline—Rule.

To my mind, he who does not help us at the needful moment, never helps; he who does not counsel at the needful moment, never counsels. I also reckon it essential that we lay down and continually impress on children certain laws, to operate as a kind of hold in life. Nay, I could almost venture to assert that it is better to be wrong by rule, than to be wrong with nothing but the fitful caprices of our own disposition to impel us hither and thither; and in my way of viewing men, there always seems to be a void in their nature, which cannot be filled up, except by some decisive and distinctly defined law.

Education and Natural Genius.

With man the first and last consideration is activity; and we cannot act on anything without the proper gifts for it, without the instinct which impels us to it. You admit that poets must be born such; you admit this with regard to all professors of the fine arts, because you must admit it, because those workings of human nature can scarce be aped with any plausibility. But, if we consider strictly, we shall find that every capability, however slight, is born with us; that there is no vague general capability in men. It is our ambiguous dissipating education that makes men uncertain: it awakens wishes when it should be animating tendencies; instead of forwarding our real capacities, it turns our efforts towards objects which are frequently discordant with the mind that aims at them. I augur better of a child, or a youth who is wandering astray along a path of his own, than of many who are walking rightly upon paths which are not theirs. If the former class, either by themselves or by the guidance of others, ever find the right path, that is to say, the path which suits their nature, they will never leave it; while the latter are in danger every moment of shaking off a foreign yoke, and abandoning themselves to unrestricted licence.

Education.

To educate their children, women should
Do as the ducks do with their plashing brood:
Swim up and down with every son and daughter—
Only, of course, to swim there must be water.

Self-Education.

How from the seed the plant may aptly grow,
The gardener is the proper man to know;
But how a youth shall grow into a man,
Each trains himself what best or worst he can.

THE END.

PRINTED BY WILLIAM BLACKWOOD AND SONS.

SELECT LIST

OF

MESSRS BLACKWOOD'S PUBLICATIONS.

LAYS AND LEGENDS OF ANCIENT GREECE. By JOHN STUART BLACKIE, Emeritus Professor of Greek in the University of Edinburgh. Second Edition. Fcap. 8vo, 5s.

"BLACKWOOD'S FOREIGN CLASSICS FOR ENGLISH READERS."

GOETHE. By A. HAYWARD, Q.C. Crown 8vo, price 2s. 6d.

"He has given us a sketch of Goethe's life; he has passed all his great works in review, giving a brief account of each, interspersed with telling extracts; and he has managed withal to furnish a running comment of just and precise criticism, so tersely expressed as almost to make us think that Mr Lewes is diffuse and Mr Carlyle extravagant. The task was a supremely difficult one, but it has been accomplished with rare success, and the effect produced is that of a cleanly cut gem which sparkles on every facet...... It is the condensed product of original and independent study, full of sound criticism, instructive comment, and piquant reflection."—*Times.*

THE STORY OF MY LIFE. By the late COLONEL MEADOWS TAYLOR, Author of 'Confessions of a Thug,' 'Tara, a Mahratta Tale,' &c. Edited by his DAUGHTER. With Preface by HENRY REEVE, C.B. Fourth and Cheaper Edition. Crown 8vo, with Coloured Frontispiece, 6s.

"The autobiography has the interest of an exciting romance, while it abounds in information and exhilarates like a tonic our entire moral nature, and gives us faith in the moral sympathies of humanity. It is a book for young men to read and study, if they would know the secret of success in life."—*British Quarterly Review.*

THE HISTORICAL PLAYS OF SHAKSPEARE. With INTRODUCTIONS and NOTES. By CHARLES WORDSWORTH, D.C.L., Bishop of S. Andrews. In 3 vols. post 8vo, 7s. 6d. each.

VOL. I. *Contents:*—CORIOLANUS—JULIUS CÆSAR—ANTONY AND CLEOPATRA—KING JOHN. VOL. II. KING RICHARD II.—KING HENRY IV., Parts I. and II.—KING HENRY V.—KING HENRY VI., *Part I. (Abridged).* VOL. III. KING HENRY VI., *Parts II. and III.*—KING RICHARD III.—KING HENRY VIII.

ANCIENT CLASSICS FOR ENGLISH READERS. Edited by the REV. W. LUCAS COLLINS, M.A. Complete in 28 volumes, price 2s. 6d. each, in cloth (sold separately); or bound in 14 vols., with calf or vellum back, for £3, 10s.

Contents:—HOMER: THE ILIAD.—HOMER: THE ODYSSEY.—HERODOTUS.— XENOPHON.— ÆSCHYLUS.— SOPHOCLES.— EURIPIDES.—ARISTOPHANES.—PLATO.—LUCIAN.—HESIOD AND THEOGNIS.—GREEK ANTHOLOGY. — VIRGIL.— HORACE.—JUVENAL.—PLAUTUS AND TERENCE.—THE COMMENTARIES OF CÆSAR.—TACITUS.—CICERO.—PLINY'S LETTERS.—LIVY. — OVID. — CATULLUS, TIBULLUS, AND PROPERTIUS. — DEMOSTHENES.—ARISTOTLE.—THUCYDIDES.—LUCRETIUS.—PINDAR.

"It is difficult to estimate too highly the value of such a series as this in giving 'English readers' an insight, exact as far as it goes, into those olden times which are so remote and yet to many of us so close."
—*Saturday Review.*

IN COURSE OF PUBLICATION.

FOREIGN CLASSICS FOR ENGLISH READERS. Edited by MRS OLIPHANT. Crown 8vo, price 2s. 6d. each.

Now ready—DANTE. — VOLTAIRE. — PASCAL. — PETRARCH.—GOETHE. — MOLIÈRE. — MONTAIGNE. — RABELAIS. — CALDERON. — SAINT SIMON. — CERVANTES. — CORNEILLE AND RACINE. — MADAME DE SÉVIGNÉ. — LA FONTAINE, and other French Fabulists.— SCHILLER. — TASSO.—ROUSSEAU.

In preparation—LEOPARDI.—ALFRED DE MUSSET.

PHILOSOPHICAL CLASSICS FOR ENGLISH READERS. Edited by WILLIAM KNIGHT, LL.D., Professor of Moral Philosophy in the University of St Andrews. In crown 8vo Volumes, with Portraits, price 3s. 6d.

Now ready—

DESCARTES.	By Professor MAHAFFY, Dublin.
BUTLER.	By Rev. W. LUCAS COLLINS, M.A.
BERKELEY.	By Professor FRASER, Edinburgh.
FICHTE.	By Professor ADAMSON, Owens College, Manchester.
KANT.	By Professor WALLACE, M.A., LL.D., Oxford.
HAMILTON.	By Professor VEITCH, Glasgow.
HEGEL.	By Professor EDWARD CAIRD, Glasgow.

In preparation—

VICO. By Professor Flint, Edinburgh.
SPINOZA. By the Very Rev. Principal Caird, Glasgow.
HOBBES. By Professor Croom Robertson, London.
HUME. By the Editor.
BACON. By Prof. Nichol, Glasgow.

WORKS OF GEORGE ELIOT. CABINET EDITION. Uniform and Complete, in 20 Volumes. Printed from a New and Legible Type, in Volumes of a convenient and handsome form, price £5. *Each Volume, price 5s., may be had separately.*

"A delightful edition of George Eliot's Works.......In size, type, and paper, everything that could be wished."—*Athenæum*.

"Nowadays publishers appear to vie with each other in giving to their reissues of books at low prices all the characteristics of true excellence; and, so far, nobody has succeeded better than Messrs Blackwood in their Cabinet Edition of George Eliot's Works........A clear and well-arranged page, fine paper, and sound binding, make this edition so good a one that it would be pronounced excellent, apart from all considerations of cost."—*Pall Mall Gazette*.

NOVELS BY GEORGE ELIOT. Cheap Editions. With Illustrations.

ADAM BEDE, 3s. 6d. THE MILL ON THE FLOSS, 3s. 6d. FELIX HOLT THE RADICAL, 3s. 6d. SCENES OF CLERICAL LIFE, 3s. SILAS MARNER, 2s. 6d. ROMOLA, with Vignette, 3s. 6d. DANIEL DERONDA, with Vignette, 7s. 6d. MIDDLEMARCH, with Vignette, 7s. 6d.

IMPRESSIONS OF THEOPHRASTUS SUCH. New Edition. Crown 8vo, 5s.

THE SPANISH GYPSY. New Edition. Crown 8vo, 5s.

JUBAL; and other Poems, Old and New. New Edition. Crown 8vo, 5s.

WISE, WITTY, AND TENDER SAYINGS, IN PROSE AND VERSE. Selected from the WORKS OF GEORGE ELIOT. Fifth Edition. Crown 8vo, 6s.

THE GEORGE ELIOT BIRTHDAY BOOK. Printed on Fine Paper, with red border, and handsomely bound, in cloth gilt, fcap. 8vo, 3s. 6d.; or in elegant leather binding, 6s.

LAYS OF THE SCOTTISH CAVALIERS, AND OTHER POEMS. By W. EDMONDSTOUNE AYTOUN, D.C.L., Professor of Rhetoric and Belles-Lettres in the University of Edinburgh. 28th Edition. Fcap. 8vo, 7s. 6d.

AN ILLUSTRATED EDITION OF THE SAME. From Designs by SIR NOEL PATON. Small 4to, 21s., in gilt cloth.

BON GAULTIER'S BOOK OF BALLADS. By W. EDMONDSTOUNE AYTOUN and SIR THEODORE MARTIN, K.C.B. Thirteenth Edition. With Illustrations by Doyle, Leech, and Crowquill. Post 8vo, gilt edges, 8s. 6d.

NERO: A HISTORICAL PLAY. By W. W. STORY, Author of 'Roba di Roma.' Fcap. 8vo, 6s.

GRAFFITI D'ITALIA. By the SAME. Second Edition. Fcap. 8vo, 7s. 6d.

THE POETICAL WORKS OF MRS HEMANS. Copyright Editions. One Volume, royal 8vo, 5s. The Same, with Illustrations engraved on Steel, gilt edges, 7s. 6d.

PATRICK HAMILTON. A Tragedy of the Reformation in Scotland, 1528. By T. P. JOHNSTON. Crown 8vo, with Two Etchings by the Author, 5s.

THE WORKS OF HORACE. Translated into English Verse, with Life and Notes. By SIR THEODORE MARTIN, K.C.B. 2 vols. post 8vo, printed on hand-made paper, 21s.

THE COMEDY OF THE NOCTES AMBROSIANÆ. By CHRISTOPHER NORTH. Edited by JOHN SKELTON, Advocate. With a Portrait of Professor WILSON and the ETTRICK SHEPHERD, engraved on Steel. Crown 8vo, 7s. 6d.

THORNDALE; or, THE CONFLICT OF OPINIONS. By WILLIAM SMITH, Author of 'A Discourse on Ethics,' &c. A New Edition. Crown 8vo, 10s. 6d.

LITTLE COMEDIES. OLD AND NEW. By JULIAN STURGIS. Enlarged Edition. Crown 8vo, 7s. 6d.

THE HISTORY OF SCOTLAND: FROM AGRICOLA'S INVASION TO THE EXTINCTION OF THE LAST JACOBITE INSURRECTION. By JOHN HILL BURTON, D.C.L., Historiographer-Royal for Scotland. New Edition, Revised, 8 vols., and Index. Crown 8vo, £3, 3s.

THE SCOT ABROAD. By the SAME. Second Edition. Complete in One volume. Crown 8vo, 10s. 6d.

SIR ARCHIBALD ALISON, BART., D.C.L.

SOME ACCOUNT OF MY LIFE AND WRITINGS.
AN AUTOBIOGRAPHY. By the late SIR ARCHIBALD ALISON, BART., D.C.L. Edited by his DAUGHTER-IN-LAW. New and Cheaper Edition. 8vo.

THE FAITHS OF THE WORLD. A CONCISE HISTORY
OF THE GREAT RELIGIOUS SYSTEMS OF THE WORLD. By Various AUTHORS. Being the ST GILES' LECTURES—Second Series. Complete in One Volume, crown 8vo, 5s.

A TOUR IN GREECE, 1880. By RICHARD RIDLEY
FARRER. With Twenty-seven full-page Illustrations, by LORD WINDSOR. Royal 8vo, with a Map, 21s.

THOMAS CARLYLE. AN ESSAY. By Major-General
SIR E. B. HAMLEY, K.C.M.G. Second Edition. Crown 8vo, 2s. 6d.

A BOOK ABOUT ROSES. By S. REYNOLDS HOLE.
With a Coloured Frontispiece by the Hon. Mrs FRANCKLIN. Seventh Edition, Revised, 7s. 6d.

MARGARET SIM'S COOKERY. With an INTRODUC-
TION by L. B. WALFORD, Author of 'Mr Smith: A Part of his Life,' 'Pauline,' and 'Cousins.' In One Volume. Crown 8vo.

PROFESSOR JOHNSTON'S CHEMISTRY OF COM-
MON LIFE. New Edition, revised and brought down to the present time. By ARTHUR HERBERT CHURCH, M.A. Oxon., Author of 'Food, its Sources, Constituents, and Uses;' 'The Laboratory Guide for Agricultural Students,' &c. Illustrated with Maps and 102 Engravings on Wood. Crown 8vo, pp. 618, 7s. 6d.

HISTORY OF THE INVASION OF THE CRIMEA.
By A. W. KINGLAKE. Cabinet Edition. Seven Volumes, crown 8vo, illustrated with Maps and Plans. 6s. each. The Volumes respectively contain :—

I. THE ORIGIN OF THE WAR.—II. RUSSIA MET AND INVADED.—III. THE BATTLE OF THE ALMA.—IV. SEBASTOPOL AT BAY.—V. THE BATTLE OF BALACLAVA.—VI. THE BATTLE OF INKERMAN.—VII. WINTER TROUBLES.

EOTHEN. By the SAME. A New Edition, uniform with
the Cabinet Edition of the 'History of the Crimean War.' 6s.

TALES FROM "BLACKWOOD." NEW SERIES. In 24 Shilling Parts. Each complete in itself, or in 12 Volumes, handsomely bound in cloth, 30s.

"These very portable little volumes may be recommended as the most engaging and unobtrusive of travelling companions."—*Times.*

"The stories are for all manner of moods and for every order of tastes."—*Athenæum.*

CONTENTS OF VOLUMES:—I. Irene Macgillicuddy, &c.—II. The Battle of Dorking, &c.—III. Who Painted the Great Murillo de la Merced? &c. —IV. The Romance of Ladybank, &c.—V. The Autobiography of a Joint-Stock Company (Limited), &c.—VI. What I did at Belgrade, &c. —VII. Cousin John's Property, &c.—VIII. The Devil's Frills: a Story of Eulenberg, &c.—IX. Guy Neville's Ghost, &c.—X. The Missing Bills: an Unsolved Mystery, &c.—XI. The Haunted Enghenio, &c.— XII. Left-handed Elsa, &c.

THE FIRST SERIES OF TALES FROM "BLACKWOOD," forming Twelve Volumes of interesting and amusing railway reading. One Shilling each in paper cover, may be had at all Railway Bookstalls.

CONTENTS OF VOLUMES:—I. The Glenmutchkin Railway, &c.—II. Lazaro's Legacy, &c.—III. A Reading Party in the Long Vacation, &c. —IV. How I Stood for the Dreeplaily Burghs, &c.—V. Adventures in Texas, &c.—VI. My Friend the Dutchman, &c.—VII. My English Acquaintance, &c.—VIII. The Surveyor's Tale, &c.—IX. Rosaura; a Tale of Madrid, &c.—X. Antonio di Carara, &c.—XI. The Natolian Story-Teller, &c.—XII. Tickler among the Thieves! &c.

THE EARLY HOMES OF PRINCE ALBERT. By ALFRED RIMMER, Author of 'Our Old Country Towns,' &c. Beautifully illustrated with Tinted Plates, and numerous Engravings on Wood. One volume, 8vo, 21s.

"Charmingly illustrated volume,......giving in a light and lively style sketches of the Prince Consort's youth and boyhood."—*Times.*

THE JEWS OF BARNOW. Stories by KARL EMIL FRANZOS. Translated by M. W MACDOWALL. Crown 8vo, 6s.

"These stories deserve great praise. They are told in a simple straightforward style, which rises at times, when the situation requires it, to a very high level.......They possess, moreover, the great charm of novelty.......It is well worthy of notice that the book has been exceptionally well translated."—*Saturday Review.*

WILLIAM BLACKWOOD & SONS, EDINBURGH AND LONDON.

www.ingramcontent.com/pod-product-compliance
Lightning Source LLC
Chambersburg PA
CBHW021204230426
43667CB00006B/551